NO PROBLEM TO MAYO AND BACK

by

Ann Lenihan

written by

Angela Phelan

BLACKWATER PRESS

ACKNOWLEDGEMENTS

We wish to acknowledge the following ;

Mr. John Daly, Managing Director of ICL who put a super computer at our disposal. His secretary Colette Keenan and Tim Phelan, who made sure we were computer literate within an hour ... no mean feat.

Mr. Dick O' Brien and his staff at the Press Office at Foreign Affairs for their endless co-operation. Ms. Peg Fogarty, Department of Defense for sourcing so many photographs.

The editors of the Irish Independent, Mr. Vincent Doyle, The Irish Times, Mr. Conor Brady, The Star, Mr. Michael Brophy, and their picture library staff without whom we would not have been able to chronicle the last two years.

Mr. Jim Farrelly, Features Editor, Irish Independent for his great support and enthusiasm for this book.

Mr. John O' Connor, Marketing Director of Folens whose encourage- ment, energy and professionalism throughout, made this project a reality (and got us out on time too).

Ms. Antoinette Higgins and Ms. Hilda O' Sullivan, our editors.

Ms. Jean Moran, Managing Director Publicity Plus, whose contribution to the project was quite invaluable.

Printed in Ireland at the press of the publishers 1990

© Blackwater Press 1990
8 Airton Road,
Tallaght,
Dublin 24.

ISBN 0 86121 124 3

Design and layout
Philip Ryan

TO THE MEDICAL STAFF OF
THE MATER HOSPITAL, DUBLIN
AND THE MAYO CLINIC, ROCHESTER, MINNESOTA,
WITHOUT WHOM THIS BOOK COULD NOT HAVE BEEN WRITTEN.

FOREWORD

On May 23rd 1989, Brian recieved a life-saving liver transplant at the Rochester Methodist Hospital, part of the famous Mayo Clinic in Minnesota.

After the operation I was inundated with questions about his illness and transplant and how we as a family coped with this illness.

This book is an attempt to answer these questions and to give hope and courage to other people with serious illnesses.

Proceeds from this book will be donated to the Kidney Transplant Foundation of Ireland whose research benefits all organ transplants.

Ann Lenihan. March 5th 1990

CHAPTER ONE

Looking back now, it seems hard to remember a time when I didn't know Brian. We both came from Athlone, where my father was a Superintendent in the Gardaí and my mother was a doctor in the town. Brian's father was the head of the Gentex company in Athlone, among other interests. Both families knew each other for years and always got on very well. Brian's mother, who was also Ann, was a great Bridge player and she and my father played regularly together. Of course Athlone was no different from other Irish towns back then in the 40's and 50's when practically everyone knew everyone else.

Brian was born in 1930 and I was born in 1937, so while back then he was never part of my own close group of friends, I knew him because I was friendly with his sisters Mary and Anne. We used to go to parties at each other's homes and when I went to Lenihans', he'd be around the place with his own friends. But I never took a lot of notice of him then. I considered him much older than our group. When we were all in secondary school, he was off in UCD studying Law. There were four children in the Lenihan family of which Brian was the eldest. In addition to the two girls, he also has a brother Paddy. In the Devine family, I was an only girl with three brothers Derry, Conor and Brendan. With so many Anns between both families, Granny Lenihan, as we all fondly called Brian's Mum, used to call me "Devine Ann", a name that stuck to me within the family over the years.

When I finished school, I went to UCG to study Dentistry. It was during holidays back home in Athlone that I started to meet Brian again. By then he was a barrister practising in Dublin. We hit it off very well together. When I went back to college again, he always seemed able to find a reason to drop down to Galway, more often than not, unexpectedly. I got used to telegrams heralding his arrival. The reason for the urgency of his communications was there was no 'phone in my digs. After a while the landlady got used to the idea that a telegram did not always mean bad news.

He was working hard trying to get his career as a barrister established then, so he didn't have too much time for courting. We went out together for about a year and a half before we became engaged. By then, I had done three years of Dentistry and it seemed the right thing for me to give it up when we got married. I was just 21. People said that I should go back and finish it. I had only two more years to my degree, but I had no real wish to go back to it. Even when, years later, we came to live in Dublin, friends thought I would finish it then. I really felt myself that I would do something in College, but not Dentistry. I feel in those days we didn't really get the appropriate career guidance, and I was also probably influenced a bit by the fact that my mother was a doctor. But with hindsight I wasn't really scientifically minded and I suppose I was very immature when I left school. After all I was only seventeen and I didn't really know what I wanted to do with my life.

Just married. August 1958.

We got married six months later in August 1958 and we started our new life together in Athlone. Brian had been elected to the Senate the previous year but he was still very much concentrating on his law career.

With the benefit of hindsight now I don't think I really understood him enough when I married him first. At 21 you think the world's your oyster and as far as I was concerned he was a barrister with a bright career. I didn't realise for some time that he was hellbent on a career in politics.

Not that he tried to cover up his political ambitions from me. He was definite that he would be very busy and that he was determined to make his life in politics. But I never really understood then what was involved. I was very apolitical, I came from a family that didn't take a great interest in politics, so this kind of lifestyle was all new to me. Also I was very young and if truth be told I suppose a bit immature then too. In those days you just went along with what your husband wanted to do and I knew I had to accept him as he was. I didn't want to try to change him, and since politics was what he passionately wanted to pursue, I was happy to support him. Now, after thirty-two years of marriage, I know that Brian would never have been content in a career that did not involve public service, because his whole life has been dedicated to serving his country and those who elected him.

Generally they were very happy times in Athlone, despite the fact that invariably, Brian was away a lot. You can imagine the life of an aspiring deputy living in Athlone and having parts of the constituency 90 miles away. Trying to cover the whole constituency didn't always leave a lot of time for the family, and I learned from the very early days that the children and the household would always be my responsibility.

But the big plus then, which made it all worthwhile, was the fact that we had all the families around us. We had my parents only down the road and Brian's father and mother only a few miles away. The many friends nearby made it a very enjoyable time in our lives. We were all very close. Four of the children were born in Athlone. Brian Jnr. was born in 1959 and a year later Mark was born. Conor was born in 1964 and Niall arrived four years later in 1968.

Brian was first elected to Dáil Éireann for the Roscommon / Leitrim constituency in 1961. On his first day in the Dáil he was appointed Parliamentary Secretary to the Minister for Lands and Fisheries by the late Taoiseach Seán Lemass. That was a red letter day for us Lenihans. We were all so proud of him, especially his father, who got an even greater kick out of Brian's new status in Dáil Éireann than when he was subsequently elected to the Dáil himself four years later.

Brian was appointed Minister for Justice in 1964 and received his Seal of Office from President Éamonn de Valera at Áras an Úachtarán. This should have been a time of great celebration for us, but it was marred by our little Mark's illness. He was only four then and he had been such a healthy baby and little boy. We never had any trouble with him.

Indeed I often used to think how lucky we were with him because he was a great eater when the other children were a bit finicky about their food. But he used to tire easily, which I couldn't understand. Of course we went through the usual routine of taking him to our doctor to see if he could make a diagnosis. But nothing was discovered.

Later we were referred to the Children's Hospital in Crumlin and after a series of tests, leukaemia was finally diagnosed. We faced the awful heart-break of knowing that his disease was incurable and there was really nothing the doctors could do to save him. He died a year later. He was only five. Naturally we were devastated because we'd had a happy family and a good life up to this, when out of the blue we got this blow. The doctors tried to ease our grief by telling us that Mark had no pain, he really didn't suffer until the last week of his life. In a way, I think you never get over the death of a child, but you have to get on with life and do the best you can. We have always had great faith in God and it helped us through our dark times then.

Life in Athlone continued much the same for us. Brian was up in Dublin for the Dáil sittings and at weekends he travelled the length and breadth of the constituency. In 1968 he was appointed Minister for Education after the sudden death of his close friend and colleague Donogh O' Malley T.D. Little did we know then that nearly twenty years later his sister Mary O' Rourke would receive the same portfolio. In 1969, he was appointed Minister for Transport and Power until 1973 when he was appointed Minister for Foreign Affairs. In the 1973 General Election, he lost his seat. Naturally he was bitterly disappointed because he had always worked so hard for Roscommon/Leitrim.

The Family.

Brian recieves his Seal of Office from President De Valera in 1964.

It seemed a good time to take stock of our lives and for Brian to consider a new direction in his career. We had recently moved to Dublin. This was a major decision for all of us. For Brian, who loved his home town and liked nothing better at weekends than to go for a long stroll out by the lake or along the banks of the Shannon. For me, it was moving away from our families and friends who had always been so supportive and also it was going to be a totally different lifestyle. In Athlone then, you never put the lock on the door, and there was always someone or other dropping in. By comparison, I knew that Dublin would be quite different.

Brian's sister Anne was living in Castleknock. We liked the idea of the big open spaces in the Phoenix Park and we thought it would be nice to move close to some of the family too. I was expecting Paul at the time and we were really pleased with our new home. While we missed both families in Athlone, it meant that the children saw a lot more of their father. Paul was born shortly after our move giving us our first Dub. in '71. And while I love all the boys dearly, I was absolutely thrilled when our only daughter Anita was born in 1973.

Meanwhile Brian didn't waste any time resuming his political career. He was a member of the European Parliament and leader of the Fianna Fáil delegation there from 1973 to 1977 and was also the leader of the opposition in the Senate. He was elected to Dublin County Council from 1974 to 1977. But the one thing he wanted more than anything else was to be back in the Dáil.

In the 1977 General Election, he stood as a candidate for Dublin West and he topped the poll. I think that still remains one of the great highlights of his political career. He was appointed Minister for Forestry and Fisheries in the new Dáil, a portfolio he retained until he was elected to Foreign Affairs for a second time in 1979. He remained at Iveagh House until 1981 when he switched to Agriculture from March 1982 to December of that year.

On September 13th 1986 Brian Jnr. got married. We were all absolutely delighted because we really liked his bride-to-be, Patricia Ryan. They were both young barristers working in Dublin and we thought how lucky we were that Brian was marrying such a nice girl and that they were going to live in Dublin after their wedding. It was a really lovely day. There wasn't a hitch from beginning to end, even the weather was glorious. The ceremony at Mount Argus was lovely and the reception afterwards was at The United Services Club in St. Stephen's Green. My memories of that day really are of the fun we had. Both families kept the guest list to families and very close friends and I can still see Granny Lenihan lecturing Charlie Haughey about something and wagging her finger at him. She was well able to have her say no matter who it was. Of course it was a very big day for Anita. She was bridesmaid and was quite apprehensive about her responsibility.

Brian was quite nervous about making his speech, which was ironic since he had made so many political speeches in his career. I remember he made a rather obscure and I thought a very religious-based speech. Though he's that kind of person, he doesn't like to get emotional at times like that. But I remember thinking how well he looked that day, how proud he was of his eldest son and indeed, of all of his family and what fine form he was in. I was also delighted because my brother Derry had flown in from South Africa for the wedding. He was Brian Jnr.'s godfather and we don't see him very often. So all in all it was a very happy time for our family. And that night , after all the celebrations were over and we were back home chatting about the events of the day, I remember saying what a great day it had been and how lucky we were with our family and friends.

When Fianna Fáil was re-elected in 1987 Brian was appointed Tánaiste and Minister for Foreign Affairs. Of all of the ministries that he had occupied over the years, I think myself, that he enjoyed Foreign Affairs the most, though he'd probably kill me for saying that. He really enjoyed every minute at Iveagh House, he had a fabulous staff there and that particular time was such an interesting and historic period to represent the Irish Government.

Now that the two younger children were almost grown up, for the first time in my life, I felt free to travel with him and to enjoy that part of his life, without worrying about what was going on at home. Yes, we all knew how lucky we were. The older children were doing well. Brian and his wife Pat were at the Bar, Conor was in London, working as a journalist, Niall was at Trinity, also studying Law while Paul was at Belvedere College and Anita was also close to home, as a day girl at Mount Sackville Convent.

So as we prepared for Christmas that year, 1987, the gods seemed to smile on us. Little did we know that in a matter of weeks, our world would be turned upside-down.

Man to man with Paul (centre) and Niall (right).

CHAPTER TWO

We were not even halfway through December when the first blow struck, leaving our whole family very distressed. Brian's driver, Garda Pat Shaughnessy had driven us for many years. We saw so much of him he became almost one of the family.

When he was going off for his week's leave we were in the kitchen having a bit of a laugh about Christmas shopping and everything that had to be done between then and the holiday. As he went out the front door, he called back "Cheerio" and I don't think I had ever seen him looking better. That was on Monday December 11th.

On the following Wednesday, Anita answered the 'phone about tea-time to be told that Pat was dead. He had died of a massive heart attack. He was only 38 years old and he had a lovely wife and two young children. They were in a total state of shock. But the only consolation then was that he wasn't driving when it happened, because so many other people would have been hurt. Our whole family was completely knocked out by the loss of such a good friend, especially Brian. Over the years they had criss-crossed the country through good times and bad and in every kind of weather. I felt that he always looked out for Brian's welfare when they were on those exhausting trips.

We all went to his funeral and my sister-in-law, Clic Devine from Naas came too because she and my brother Conor were extremely fond of Pat. Conor is a doctor in Naas and both our families have always been very close. They have children much the same ages as ours and between our visits to them and their visits to us in town they would have met Pat frequently over the years. Conor was particularly upset because he couldn't rearrange his surgery to attend the funeral. After the funeral Clic went home to Naas and though she never said anything to me at the time, she told Conor that she had got an awful shock when she saw Brian. Even though it was only a few weeks since we had been with them,

Minister for Agriculture (1982).

she thought he looked simply dreadful. She thought it might be the shock of Pat's death that had given him such an awful pallor so she told Conor to 'phone Brian immediately to see if he felt alright.

Since they were coming to us with their children a couple of days later during the holidays, Conor felt that he could check out Brian himself then. At that stage they didn't say anything to me about their concern. Isn't it funny that when you're very close to someone, seeing them day in, day out, that you don't really notice a change in them as much as other people do ? While Brian didn't look well that day, I put it down to his grief at the loss of his friend and of course he had a particularly hectic schedule at work at that time , so there seemed good enough reason that he wouldn't have been in tiptop form.

But when Conor and Clic and the family arrived on Stephen's Day, Conor too was shocked by Brian's appearance. He got him to

Proud father-in-law

lie down on the floor of the drawing-room to check him out and his immediate reaction was that Brian should go into hospital for a thorough examination. I thought it was typical of Brian to opt to go into hospital immediately after Christmas. But after so many years of being married to him, I knew his reasons only too well. With the Dáil on Christmas recess, he would be able to nip in and out without missing a single day of work. So in January we packed all the bits and pieces necessary for a few days in hospital and Brian went into the Mater Private Nursing Home.

Neither of us was particularly apprehensive about the prospect of his hospitalization. If anything, he himself was quite relieved to be going in for what he thought would be little more than a routine check. Diabetes was subsequently diagnosed but the doctors also felt there was a possible problem with his liver. He was put on a very strict diet with absolutely no alcohol, which we thought was a bit of a joke since Brian , being the social animal that he is, always loved his few drinks.

The doctors felt that the liver problem might well solve itself if this extremely rigid diet regime was strictly adhered to. Brian was adamant that he would do what he was told and abide by the draconian schedule that had been drawn up by his doctors for him. So when he started to lose weight we didn't panic, because we were told that this was all part of controlling the diabetes. The doctors hoped that within a few months he would be able to pace himself and gauge his medication and he really did make an all-out effort. But his progress was very up and down. He would improve a bit and then he would get an unexpected set-back. From having gone in just for a check-up, during the next three weeks, as the doctors continued to run every possible kind of test on him, it was now becoming clear that he was in fact far more seriously ill than we ever imagined.

The doctors at the Mater still put it all in context saying that he could improve by doing everything he was told. He would have to face up to a new lifestyle. Meals would have to be taken regularly, and more than anything, he would have to try to get more rest. And I can tell you that trying to get Brian Lenihan to rest was one very tall order indeed. To that end, while he was in the Mater, his doctors ordered that he should have no visitors. So except for immediate family he had a very quiet time. Charlie Haughey and some of the other ministers 'phoned him to wish him well. Brian and Charlie have been the very best of friends for well over thirty years and Charlie told me of his concern for Brian's health and he told me to try to get Brian to take things a bit easier. Talk of preaching to the converted on that occasion! In Leinster House as well as in Iveagh House they were all surprised to hear of his illness too, because as one of them said to me, "There are men half his age who can't keep up with him." He has always been a very hard worker.

A word of advice from Granny to Charlie.

The doctors and nurses were fantastic not only to Brian but to me as well. The third floor nurses, with Sister Mercy in charge, thoroughly spoiled him and the chefs and cooks were serving up Cordon Bleu meals regularly. Despite the worries and tensions there was always fun and repartee between him and his wonderful staff. His medication was revised. But now the doctors were beginning to be concerned by the results of the tests they had already run on his liver. They felt that if they were to investigate his liver any further, they would have to perform a biopsy and they told me that they considered this a huge risk, a last resort, and to be avoided for the present. When he began to make steady progress yet again a few days later his doctors felt that by taking the exact medication and above all by doing what he was told that he could well improve himself in time.

During all of these complications and set-backs I was in total shock, shock like I have never experienced before. After all Brian had rarely been sick a day in his life, he had always enjoyed robust good health and he always seemed to have virtually endless energy for life. He was a great eater, he loved nothing better than a big juicy steak. But, unlike me, he could also go without food all day long if he was busy, or if he was travelling. He was able to put in all kinds of ungodly hours working in the office, often way past midnight. Yet he would be up at the crack of dawn to catch a flight to some EEC meeting, having been fully briefed prior to departure. I suppose the fact that he loved his work so much and had such a tremendous enthusiasm for it all helped him through that period.

But there were times when I often wondered how he was able to motivate himself, when I knew he wasn't feeling well. The thing about Brian that impressed not only our family, but everyone who looked after him during his illness, was that from first to last he never once complained. He has always been the eternal optimist. So he too felt that by obeying his new regime, he would get the diabetes under control and possibly everything else would go right as well then. Even though he did lose a lot of weight at that time, he was feeling fine when he was discharged three weeks later.

In one way, it did change his life somewhat. He observed everything the doctors had ordered to the absolute letter of the law, because he wanted to continue his work without any further set-backs. He began to take his meals at regular times and he was very careful about what he would eat. If he couldn't get home for lunch or dinner, I would often come into town to meet him, because unknowingly he might eat something sweet and also I have to admit that I was still very worried about him and I was desperately protective of him. I was particularly protective about his appearance, because he had got so thin and frail. As he continued to lose weight, I was constantly running backwards and forwards to the tailors having his suits taken in. And I replaced most of his shirts too, because he was now taking a much smaller collar size, smaller than any of his sons, quite a change from a robust size 17.

People tell me now, just how awful Brian looked then, and looking back at photographs taken during the eighteen months of his illness, of course I can see it now. But it didn't really have an impact on me then, because, I suppose you try to get your mind to block out what you don't want to accept. But Brian himself never let it get to him. Of course well-meaning people would often ask him how he was feeling. But you know Brian, his reply was always, " Oh fine, I'm on the mend now, business as usual. No problem." But I know that while he kept up a very brave face, he often felt hurt by the way people looked at him and I remember one evening when he came home, he said, " Why do people look at me like that, Ann, I really hate those looks." However the major thing for him was that despite everything, he was back at work which he enjoyed so much and that he felt able to do his job well.

But the tiredness continued to come and go when he came home from hospital and I think he found that most frustrating. The reality seemed to be that he wasn't getting better as time went on as he dearly hoped and prayed for. He was never a person to have great patience for looking after himself. When he continued to get these weaknesses and collapsed again, he felt very frustrated indeed because he didn't want to be out of work and more than anything else he so badly wanted to be healthy.

Of course the family knew that he was ill. Brian Jnr. and his wife, Patricia were living over on the south side of Dublin and they would see him quite regularly. Niall, Paul and Anita saw him at home everyday, so they didn't notice the dramatic change. It was Conor, who would meet Brian when he was in London for meetings of the Anglo-Irish Conference, who would see a big

Fig 2.4 Election victory, February 1987.

change in him. I didn't want to alarm them too much by telling them that the doctors were worried about Brian's liver as well as the diabetes, and besides none of us knew anything more at that point anyway. There was no point in having them worrying about their father, when we felt then that the signs were that he was gradually recovering. Brian had enough to do getting on with his job without having the whole family hysterical with worry. He would have hated nothing more than that.

After all, this was one of the busiest times ever for him as Minister of Foreign Affairs. In addition to all of the ongoing business at the Department, there were Anglo-Irish Meetings, there was the usual run of EEC Meetings, there were United Nations Meetings and there was a lot of activity in the United States, lobbying on behalf of the Irish illegals and actively seeking more visas in Washington. Brian also had his constituency work to attend to and this was always a priority with him. This was a very busy time. But even when he would come in late at night from some local meetings, the 'phone never stopped ringing and the doorbell seemed to have a life of its own, especially at weekends. However no matter who it was, or at what time of the night, Brian always had time to talk. Though I don't mind admitting there were times I could have killed him, because he simply wasn't able to burn the candle at both ends then.

And as if all that wasn't enough, the Government had already started the forward planning for Ireland's Presidency of Europe in January 1990. This would be the joint responsibility of Foreign Affairs and the Taoiseach's Department, and Brian was already eagerly looking forward to that extremely exciting six-month period when Ireland would assume the Presidency and such a busy agenda would have to be addressed. He was also looking forward to the informal meetings with his fellow ministers from Europe, many of whom had become good friends and to having an opportunity to show them a bit of the Irish countryside. Brian and I had often joked about what always happens to the best laid plans, because so often over the years we have had to cancel plans for an evening out or even holidays because of his work. But who could have predicted then that Brian would be at death's door before that Presidency would commence in Dublin, less than 18 months later.

On yer bike! May 1986.

In pensive mood, Árd Fheis 1987.

Big Brian goes Country and Western.

CHAPTER THREE

By May Brian's health had really declined. Despite the fact that he was under constant observation by the medical team in the Mater, he just didn't seem to be getting his energy back. In fact during May '88 he collapsed again and was readmitted to the Mater to have his whole case reassessed.

That was the first time that I think the whole illness really got to him. He thought that everything should have gone smoothly after January, but in fact it didn't. So when he collapsed in May, he was really very unwell and he began to think that if he had to keep going into hospital every few months to get sorted out, he wouldn't be able to do his job properly and that he should retire. He had put in a very difficult few months. On a number of occasions, luckily they all happened at home, he became very weak. I would ring the Mater frantic with worry and they were

Conor and Clic Devine.

Ireland 1 : England 0. Celebrating at Stuttgart.

really very good to us. They would tell me to get him into the hospital as quickly as possible and once they had him in for a few days, they were able to sort out his problem, which still seemed to be diabetes, and get him on his feet again.

While he had a few set-backs during that time, I never thought that he was really ill because he kept working at such a rate. But I was very nervous after the initial diagnosis in January. I was nervous about his workload, I was nervous about all the travelling, I was nervous about his diet. In a nutshell, I was a nervous wreck at that time. The funny thing was that Brian himself was not nervous then, or at any stage of his illness. I found that very hard to understand but I suppose I should have known the will-power

Welcome home.

Keeping it in the family.

of the man. He is a religious person, he really has incredibly strong faith. His mother was a very religious woman too and I'd say he must have inherited that staunch faith somewhere in his family. Every cloud has a silver lining, they say, and Brian's illness brought us much closer together. We had always been close, but after January, I wanted to spend as much time as I could with him. I just didn't want not to be there for him.

Whereas before perhaps he would be going somewhere and I would say "Well, I'll just stay at home", this time it was imperative that I went with him. I felt that I had to go everywhere, all the time. Perhaps for the first time in his life he didn't resent me being there all the time. I know that no man wants his wife virtually shadowing him, but he didn't resent it. So it's possible that by having me there all the time, he did show a slight nervousness. But he often said how much he liked having me around. And as I said before, we became much closer as a result of being together so much.

It was a big change for me because suddenly everything became secondary to Brian. All my own activities just had to take second place. I was involved in some charity work and of course the family took up most of my time. Suddenly I didn't see as much of them, since I was jumping up at a moment's notice to go out. I think any mother will agree it isn't easy when you have young children. I must say the children coped very well. They became very much more self-sufficient about minding themselves, getting their meals and doing the practical everyday things around the house. While in one way I think it was good for them, I know it was lonely for them too, especially for the younger ones.

So though he was back in the Mater again that May, the doctors still held out hope that he would improve. They still felt it was a question of time. But they also felt that he had worked so hard since January, they could see that he had really given it everything, that they considered a good long break coming into the summer might really put him on the right road.

Co-Chairmen of the Anglo-Irish Conference

The Taoiseach came to see him and he had a long chat with him. Possibly for the first time in their lives it wasn't about politics. He was very worried about Brian and he was upset when he heard him say that he was considering retirement. Charlie insisted that what he really needed was a good long rest and that we should go over to our home in Ballyconeely in Connemara for a couple of weeks. But Brian didn't want to go over to the West. He was happy to stay at home. The weather that late May and June was beautiful and we went for long walks in Phoenix Park every day. The children were still at school so the house was quiet and Brian spent much of his time reading and he also did a bit of writing. He totally switched off work, again possibly for the first time in his life and he was completely relaxed.

At the Anglo-Irish talks are (from left to right) Justice Minister Gerry Collins, Brian , Tom King, N.I. Secretary and Ian Stewart, N.I. Minister.

Later that summer we went over to Connemara and he was improving every day. Over in the West he played a bit of golf, he wouldn't be a serious golfer or anything, but he would go to the club and hit a few balls with the children. He spent much of his time walking around there. He's always loved that part of Ireland and he's repeatedly said his idea of a perfect holiday is walking around Connemara. He also loves going out in the boat and, if he was lucky, catching a few fish. He loved chatting to the local

2

Carving up the Continental Shelf with Sir Geoffrey Howe.

fishermen and in the evening we would go to one of the hotels for dinner with friends. We were all thrilled with the great progress he was making. August seemed to fly by and he continued to improve steadily.

So by the time we were back in Dublin in September, his doctors were very pleased with him and he was delighted to go back to work. Soon it was a case of packing the bags again and we went off to a meeting of the General Assembly of the United Nations in New York. It was a particularly long visit because he had to go down to Washington for a few days too. But he seemed well able to get through all the meetings. Though it was a very busy trip, he was in great form when we arrived home at the beginning of October.

Brian and Ray Burke, Energy Minister, at the funeral mass for Pádraig Ó hAnnracháin in St. Fintan's Church, Sutton.

Greeting an old friend, Senator Ted Kennedy with Ben Briscoe.

With the Dáil open again at the end of October, we settled into as normal a routine as we've ever had. There were many trips to EEC meetings in Europe, as well as several visits to London and Belfast for the Anglo-Irish Conference. For security reasons I didn't travel with him to Belfast, but I went to as many of the other meetings as I could.

Brian's mother died at the end of November. Even though she was in her eighties, we were all upset by our loss. But we were consoled by the fact that she had such an active life and had been playing good Bridge up to three weeks before she died. She worried so much about Brian's health during his illness. She would often 'phone me to ask if there was any news about him that we were keeping from her. She had great faith and devotion to

In swinging form with , (from left to right) Stephen Roche, Christy O' Connor Junior and Éamonn Darcy. December 1988.

Padre Pio and during those long months when Brian wasn't getting better, I knew that she was storming heaven's doors with prayers for him.

Christmas came and went and though we all felt sad about Granny Lenihan, we had a good holiday that year with all the family, friends and neighbours coming and going. We felt that we had much to celebrate, Brian looked much better and seemed to be getting back to his old form. He didn't seem to tire as much as he had been, and he was pacing himself well at work. He was eating his meals at regular times but we still had a job to try to get him to rest more.

So as we faced into the New Year in 1989, I thought the worst was over. I was still a bit apprehensive, but I did feel that Brian was finally getting better and that life might return to normal for all of us again. We really felt that we were indeed the Lucky Lenihans as we started 1989.

Our man in the Park. January 1st 1989

Exchanges with the Boss at the Árd Fheis

Chairing the inaugural meeting of the Ireland and France Bicentenary Committee at Iveagh House, The group picture from left to right is(back), Dr. Frank O' Reilly, Joseph Lynch, Ciaran McGonigal (secretary), Doireann Ní Bhriain, Dr. Hugh Gough and Prof. Brendan Devlin. (Front), Joe Mulholland, Prof. Barbara Wright, Padraig Ó hUiginn (Vice chairman), Brian Lenihan (chairman), Lydia Roche and John Cooney.

CHAPTER FOUR

Starting the New Year of 1989, Brian's diary in the office was packed with meetings and appointments, mostly abroad, for the best part of the next six months, and as far as he was concerned, each meeting had its own vital importance that required him to be present there personally.

I really will never be able to say enough about the superb staff he had at Iveagh House. His Minister of State, Sean Calleary, his Private Secretary Orla O'Hanrahan, the Secretary of the Department Noel Dorr, his Press Secretary Dick O'Brien and all his people were delighted to see him back at work. I have to single out for special mention one of his secretaries, Gabriel Burke. Quite frankly, I don't think I could have got through the whole ordeal as well as I did without her tremendous help, cheerfulness and her unceasing kindness and understanding to me. And when the move to America had to be made, Gabriel's pivotal part in everything there was inestimable. She volunteered to accompany us to the Mayo Clinic and like ourselves, she had no idea what was likely to be involved in our stay there, or how long she would be away from home.

People ask me how Brian coped with his work-load then, and if he was really up to the rigorous regime that was required of him as Minister for Foreign Affairs and Tánaiste. My own answer would be that if anything he actually worked harder then to prove, to himself as much as to everyone else, that this illness was not affecting his work. But rather than give my version, we agreed it would be more accurate if Brian detailed some aspects of his own activity.

Brian

It's rather ironic that the eighteen months of my illness were definitely the most interesting of my three periods as Foreign Minis-

ter. It was a satisfying time, because I felt there was a lot happening in the international area that was important, and as a Government we were turning the economy around on the home front. In all I made over sixty visits during this term.

Although I had several set-backs, I still kept myself psyched up to do the best job possible at Foreign Affairs. It certainly became a question of mind over matter for me. It was frustrating at times because while my mind was sharp, even sharper than before, I would say, I lacked my customary energy, and so had to make the really big effort. However, I thought that by sticking to the prescribed medical regime everything would come right in time. The new lifestyle to which I have become accustomed grew on me gradually. The big thing was to eat meals, and take medicines at specified times. As for alcohol, it was out. Many people have asked me whether I miss it: the answer quite truthfully is that I don't. I still enjoy company over a drink, except that now I'm on mineral water. It doesn't upset me when I see other people drinking when I know I can't. In fact I get a vicarious pleasure from the presence of friends who are enjoying a drink. Anyway, it's a small price to pay for being alive and healthy.

It was a particularly active time in the European Community with Summits in Brussels, Copenhagen, Hanover and Rhodes, and other meetings in different European centres. The dominant theme was the Single European Act, and the creation of a Single Internal Market by 1992, linked with a doubling of structural funds for the less well-off regions of the community. The plan for this purpose was prepared by Jacques Delors, President of the Commission, and became known as the Delors Plan. It was of vital importance to Ireland, and was the crunch issue at the Summit in Copenhagen from 3rd to 5th December, 1987 attended by the Taoiseach and myself. The Germans and French came together in a strong axis. Kohl, Mitterand and the Taoiseach were for the Plan, and the United Kingdom was eventually reduced to a minority of one.

At Áras an Uachtarán with President Hillery.

With Dr. Maeve Hillery.

At Bodenstown.

Leaving Leinster House.

After a late night sitting it was proposed that a mechanism known as "stopping the clock" be adopted. This is a ploy used at these meetings when they fail to get unanimity. The clock was stopped, metaphorically speaking, and the meeting was not closed, but merely adjourned to Brussels in early February . At the February meeting, Mrs. Thatcher finally relented and agreed to the Delors Plan and the target year of 1992. It was a great triumph for Jacques Delors and the Franco-German entente. It was also a great day for us.

At the Vatican with Pope John Paul II.

Ambassador Brendan Dillon escorts us to the Vatican.

People often ask me what Margaret Thatcher is really like, and whether she lives up to her reputation as the Iron Lady. She is undoubtedly a strong-minded woman, who concentrates on her brief, but sometimes, I think, in too narrow a manner. It is a feature of the way business is done at European meetings that often important decisions are agreed over lunch or dinner, or at some of the informal meetings where there is an atmosphere of collective collegiality between Ministers and Heads of State or Government. The British Prime Minister has tended to isolate herself from this process of collective collegiality, which makes the system work. I must say that at times she has a sense of humour. I remember an occasion when she wore a smart emerald green suit, which was very flattering on her. I complimented her on how well she looked, and her immediate reply was "The Irish don't have a monopoly on green, Mr. Lenihan." Touché.

Brian with, (left), Ambassador McKeirnan and (right), Congressman Peter Rodino.

(Left), Speaker Tim Wright and (right) Ambassador MacKeirnan.

The reality however is that corridor diplomacy, smoke-filled rooms, or whatever, sometimes work, even if it isn't Mrs. Thatcher's way of doing business. I remember an informal lunch of Foreign Ministers where we were trying to decide on the cultural capital for Europe in 1991. Budapest was in line for it because there was some sympathy for the democratic direction in which Hungary was moving. Before lunch, Geoffrey Howe had been talking about Burke, Goldsmith and Swift, and during the meal we moved through the whole gamut of Anglo-Irish literature to Wilde, Shaw and Yeats, so that when I put Dublin forward as a suitable location, Howe moved in behind me, others followed suit, and before we rose from the table, Dublin was selected as cultural capital for 1991.

One of the meetings I still remember best, because it turned out to be so prophetic, was my meeting with the Pope when in Rome in June 1987 to lodge Ireland's accession document to the Single European Act. The Pope stressed the need for the Community to be sensitive to the reawakening that was taking place in his native Poland, and in Eastern Europe generally. He felt that young and educated people saw the failure of Marxism, and that change would come about through the churches. He was keen that the Community would support confidence-building measures in Eastern Europe in the areas of human rights, freedom of worship, speech and movement.

Hans-Dietrich Genscher, the German Foreign Minister spoke in a similar vein regularly at the European Political Co- operation meetings. He is a Lutheran from Halle, and has a gut feel for the evolving situation in that part of the world. Like the Pope, he also felt that the changes would come from the young and the educated and would be focused through the Catholic and Lutheran churches.

The British and Americans tended to doubt the validity of these views. Looking back now on recent events, and the maelstrom of change that has occurred throughout Eastern Europe, I find it quite remarkable how prescient and wise these two men were. Bilateral meetings and conversations are a feature of modern diplomacy. Easy communications bring Ministers together more often, and accelerate this process. I remember a Brussels Council meeting where Howe and I had differed on several matters. We decided afterwards it was time for us to agree on something which might be of mutual benefit to our two countries. We came up with the division of areas of the Continental Shelf in the North Atlantic off the British and Irish coasts.

Discussing Euro politics with Hans Dietrich Genscher in Bonn, 1988.

This had been a prolonged dispute, heading for expensive international arbitration, which might have cost over £20 million to resolve, with the possibility of an unsatisfactory outcome. Instead we settled for an Agreement signed by Howe and myself in Dublin on 7th November 1988. The result was that Ireland secured a large increase in sea-bed jurisdiction, with full economic rights of exploitation in respect of marine, mineral and other resources covering over 500,000 square miles. There are immense prospects for development when technology makes it possible at a future date.

I had an important bilateral meeting with Douglas Hurd, then Home Secretary in London in late 1988 when I first sensed British misgivings about the Guildford Four. They will have to follow suit in the case of the Birmingham Six if they are to be consistent because the injustice is equally manifest. There were of course frequent meetings of the Anglo-Irish Conference co-chaired by Tom King and myself. From the start we had a working relationship. We agreed to disagree on some aspects, but worked hard on other aspects of potential agreement.

We tidied up the rules governing the display of flags and emblems, and the holding of parades and demonstrations in Northern Ireland. The Police Authority was instituted, and security co-operation on the Border was made more effective on the ground. Economic and social matters were addressed, and funding was secured, on a North-South basis and in disadvantaged areas.

My flagship project, the waterway link between the Erne and Shannon navigation systems, is now under way. Apart from the symbolism of the link, it will provide a magnificent leisure facility for inland cruising in a most picturesque part of our island. The jobs discrimination of $2^1/_2$ to 1 against Catholics in Northern Ireland is blatantly unjust, and I insisted on priority for this matter at Conference meetings. King agreed, and so we now have Fair Employment Legislation from 1st January 1990. A new Commission is being established with powers to investigate, monitor, and enforce Fair Employment practices. Given the resources and the political will, which is a test of British bona fides, the Commission should redress what has been an intolerable wrong.

The last meeting I attended was on 5th April 1989 in Belfast, when we finalised the three year review document on the working of the Agreement, which recommends the scope of the Conference work to include other Ministers, and other areas of common social and economic interest to the whole of Ireland, particularly in a European framework.

With Jacques Delors, President of the European Commission.

With Chancellor Helmut Kohl.

With François Mitterand.

With Margaret Thatcher.

In Washington during September/October 1988 our friends in Congress were very helpful in sorting out the visa and status problems of Irish emigrants. The Donnelly visas were extended pending the enactment of the Kennedy-Simpson legislation now before Congress, which provides a permanent quota for Irish emigrants, based on a system of points for education and training. Brian Donnelly and Speaker Foley in the House and Senators Kennedy and Simpson in the Senate sponsored matters for us.

On the administration side Ambassador Heckler and then Vice-President Bush rowed in as well. I had several meetings in Washington, concerning landing rights in Los Angeles, and I am happy to say that these rights have now been granted to Aer Lingus. I flew out to the West Coast for talks on investment in Ireland. In California the emphasis was on high tech. electronics and computers. Part of the brief included companies such as Intel, who have since decided to invest here. The thrust of the message was that a location in Ireland was a gateway to the huge Single Market that would be a reality by 1992. Back to New York and an historic meeting of the United Nations General Assembly. Reagan and Shevardnadze were very positive on arms control. I was proud of the acknowledgment made by the Secretary-General to the troop-contributing nations on receiving the Nobel Prize for U.N. peace-keeping missions over the years. Ireland had been involved in every one of them. A unique distinction.

In Paris at the end of that year, the 50th anniversary of the Declaration of Human Rights was commemorated. Lech Walesa and Sakharov were introduced by Mitterand - poor Sakharov, who has since died, spoke beautifully. I was reminded of Boris Pasternak and the shadows of Dr. Zhivago - the indomitable will of the human spirit to survive and burn brighter - the recurring theme through Russia's benighted history. Early in 1989 the Vienna talks on East-West detente reached conclusions within the CSCE framework for the whole of Europe. These conclusions, dealing with Economic Co-operation, Human Rights and fundamental freedom, and Arms Control, are under *current examination in Vienna. Current developments in Central and Eastern Europe add further impetus to this process of peace and democratisation.*

I paid an official visit to Canada in March 1989. There is great scope for additional trade and investment between Canada and Ireland. Ann and I stayed with Prime Minister Brian Mulroney and his wife, and I think we helped to strengthen bilateral relations. One immediate bonus was that we signed an agreement to enable films to be made on a reciprocal tax-exemption basis. It was also heartening to take the salute at the St. Patrick's Day Parade in Toronto in which Orange and Green bands and clubs participated in full zest. Some Dubs were the catalysts on the Committee who brought this about. A sign of the future !

Freedom of the city of West Berlin.

Fellow Foreign Ministers of the Commission, Copenhagen 1987.

With Roy Hattersley, the deputy leader of the Labour Party.

Welcoming Geoffrey Howe to Iveagh House.

Good friend, Congressman Brian Donnelly.

Theatricals with Michael Colgan, of the Gate Theatre.

At the Bolshoi Ballet.

Árd Fheis hype, February 1989.

With Mila Mulroney in Ottowa, March 1989.

With the two Brians and Mila Mulroney, St. Patrick's Day, 1989.

In Boston with Mayor Ray Flynn.

Promoting Ireland with Governor Michael Dukakis.

Addressing the 42nd assembly of the United Nations, 1987.

Glasnost at the U.N. with Shevardnadze,1987.

CHAPTER FIVE

I think that Brian really considered himself blessed at the start of 1989 and he threw himself back into his work as though he had never been ill. For the first few months everything went well for him, but during our visit to Canada for St. Patrick's Day, I thought that he looked really ghastly. We had a very busy schedule in Toronto and Ottawa and the weather was -30 degrees. It was that awful cold that would chill you to the bone. I worried about Brian being outside in such awful weather, though he was well wrapped-up from the cold. On St. Patrick's Day he stood for hours reviewing the Parade. He never once complained. But I thought he didn't seem to have quite the same energy as he had had only a few weeks before and I was very glad when we arrived back from Canada safe and sound. It was always so reassuring to be at home and close to his doctors, because no matter what time of the day or night I phoned them at the Mater, they were always there for us.

'Wearing of the Green'.
Toronto 1989.

Snowbirds, Ottawa 1989.

With the Mounties.

Tip O' Neill

We were all looking forward to Easter. I felt that if Brian had another break from work that it would help to build him up again, as his break the previous summer had done. I knew that he was exceptionally busy since that break. He had deputised for the Taoiseach during his illness in October and November and there was never a week that he didn't have some overseas travel. There was still a lot of travelling to be done throughout the country here at home. Brian always likes to quote Tip O' Neill about elections, "Every election is a local election", he has always maintained that no matter how much great work you are doing for the country abroad, the people here at home want plenty of your time too. And he was trying so hard to be everywhere with everyone.

Our Easter break never materialised because of the historic visit of Mikhail Gorbachev to Shannon on April 2nd. Brian was very excited about the meeting which in addition to the Soviet leader, would be attended by their Foreign Minister Shevard-nadze, whom he had met at the United Nations on several occasions.

He was in really fine form when he headed off that Sunday. It was a bitterly cold, clear morning at Shannon and I was amused to see Charlie and himself walking out to the steps of the Soviet 'plane, neither one of them wearing an overcoat, despite the fact that they had both been very ill. And I was even more amused when the Russians, led by Gorbachev, emerged wearing top coats, scarves, mufflers and hats. When you think of the sub-zero weather they had left in Moscow, Shannon was summer-like by comparison. But they weren't taking any chances. Brian was very impressed by Gorbachev and his grasp of Irish affairs.

Brian

My personal impressions were that Gorbachev was a fascinating man whom you could relate to very quickly. He was a vital man with quite an amazing intellect. He was obviously well briefed, and didn't need to refer to any documentation during our meeting.

Once again, I was conscious of the fact that the Russians are part of the mainstream of European culture. Gorbachev has often spoken about his own religious background, about his mother's capacity for prayer to her icons, and that sort of thing. He grew up in the kind of rural environment that wouldn't have been much different from other European regions. The Pope from Kracow, and Jacques Delors from France came from similar backgrounds. His attention to detail was shown in his knowledge of the Shannon area, which he had gathered from Shevardnadze, his Foreign Minister, who stops off regularly at the airport, and tours the neighbouring hinterland out to the Cliffs of Moher and the Burren while staying over at Dromoland Castle.

The Soviet Union is already doing valuable business in Shannon, servicing and maintaining their flights and aircraft. Aer Rianta is well up and running with retail shop facilities in Moscow and Leningrad airports and more to come. The Russians were keen, as we were, to explore new economic and cultural links between our two countries. Our economic people are now pursuing a number of trade and joint

Soviets in Shannon.

Soviets in Shannon.

3

Soviets in Shannon.

Soviets in Shannon.

venture possibilities and a Cultural Agreement is now ready for signature. While there is a huge untapped market in the Soviet Union, they still have a major foreign exchange problem. Like other Eastern European countries, they will need capital investment and trade to raise their standard of living. But in the Russians' case, enterprise has been stultified by centuries of Czarist rule. Hungary, Czechoslovakia, Poland and East Germany had market economies until the 1940's and so can change over more quickly.

A light moment with Dr. Alois Moch, Austrian Vice Chancellor.

DeGaulle originally spoke about a Europe "from the Atlantic to the Urals" and Gorbachev has advocated a common European home. The Taoiseach now talked about the same Europe quoting "from the Volga to the Shannon" and was warmly applauded. Gorbachev loved it -- he and the Taoiseach got on very well together. They seemed to enjoy the same sense of humour, and had the same approach to getting the business done. When the Taoiseach briefed him on the Northern Ireland situation and the Anglo-Irish Agreement, he had a full grasp of all the complexities involved. What struck me most about the Gorbachevs was how relaxed he and his wife were. There was nothing ponderous about them, and I would sum him up very much as a modern European, who could take charge of affairs in any situation anywhere.

Some days later, Alois Moch, Foreign Minister of Austria, came to Dublin to present his country's case for full membership of the European Community. Significantly and symbolically, he presented a book to me on Charles V, the Holy Roman Hapsburg Emperor of the sixteenth century, who ruled a substantial part of Europe in civilised style from his capital, Vienna. Looking back now, I would say I was really pushing myself then, but I was still convinced that it was a case of mind over matter. However, events were to overtake me quicker than I thought.

Ann

Brian collapsed about ten days later and he was again rushed back into the Mater. This time his doctors felt they had no option but to perform the dreaded biopsy. They told me it had now become vital that they take this radical course. They outlined the dangers to me, they were afraid of excessive bleeding during the surgery. But they now had no choices left. They felt that they had explored every other avenue with no success. They felt that at 58 he was too young and had too much good service left to give, to be as constantly ill as he had been for nearly eighteen months. Now there was a new urgency about Brian's precarious state of health. The biopsy finally produced a diagnosis, which was the good news. But the bad news was the nature of that diagnosis.

Brian was discovered to be suffering from a very rare liver disorder called haemochromatosis, which is an excess of iron in the liver. It is an inherited disease, that has been found to skip a generation, so there would never be a question of the children getting it, though their children might. Brian had spent fifty-eight years building up that iron content which was doing so much damage to his liver, that his doctors felt it might now be well beyond repair.

Dr. John Lennon and Dr. Dick Firth, who had been looking after Brian from day one, met me in the Mater to discuss the options open to us and they told me that we would have to go to one of the world's specialist hospitals for further treatment. Dr. Firth is a Mayo man himself and has personal contacts with the Mayo Clinic and he felt that Brian might stand a better chance there because if he went to England, he would undoubtedly have received more headlines than he was able for. Also, it was felt that America had more privacy to offer him and that there could be security problems for an English hospital trying to look after an Irish Foreign Minister.

The doctors discussed all the options with Brian. They outlined the possible course of treatment that could be available to him and they also told him about the possibility of a liver transplant. Dr. Lennon was anxious that he would go for the liver transplant from the outset. But he was worried that Brian might not be accepted because of his age and health. Brian's immediate reaction was " I'll go for the transplant, no problem." He wasn't afraid of the prospect of such a huge operation. He felt if the transplant was going to make him better, then the sooner he got it the better. But I was very shocked. I couldn't believe that the diagnosis could have been so serious. And it was very serious because the doctors wanted me to start making plans for our departure immediately.

I went home to tell the children that we would be going to America. They didn't realise just how ill their father was, so it was a very big shock for all of them. I don't think I told them of the

Dr. John Lennon.   *Dr. Dick Firth.*   *Dr. John Crowe*

possibility of a liver transplant immediately. I was still trying to get used to the idea myself. I still consoled myself with the thought that when we arrived in Mayo, the doctors there might yet prescribe treatment. I told my brother Conor, a doctor himself in Naas and he came to meet the doctors. Once he had been told what was involved, he called the Mayo Clinic to see what the situation was there. I knew nothing about Mayo and the one thing on my mind was that we wouldn't be able to afford to go there.

I met with the Voluntary Health Insurance and they told me what cover they would extend . But Mayo had quoted the cost of a liver transplant at from $125,000 to $250,000 depending on how long you have to wait for a liver, how straightforward the surgery is and how quickly you recover afterwards. Obviously any set-backs, or worst of all rejection of the new liver, which would necessitate another transplant, would all send the costs rocketing. There were so many intangibles that you couldn't put an overall cost on it. I met with our solicitor and bank manager, I even thought of selling the house, but thankfully we didn't need to do that. A group of our friends made a contribution which made it possible for us to go there and not to have to worry about the cost. We were both very grateful to them, not simply because of the money, but because they felt that Brian had worked for the country for virtually his whole life, and they felt that he should be able to receive the best treatment that would ensure several more years of the service he so badly wanted to contribute. We are not a wealthy family and we all realise what a life-saving opportunity was afforded us.

The Taoiseach came over to the Mater to see me and I told him what the diagnosis was and of the decision to go to America. He couldn't have been more supportive. He told me not to worry about anything other than getting Brian to America as quickly as possible and to make sure we had the very best doctors there. He assured me that if we needed anything, that I simply had to give him a call. That was very reassuring indeed.

Once the decision to go to America was taken, things started to move very quickly. The doctors wanted a few days to build Brian up for the long journey. They had already decided that he was far too ill to make the trip by scheduled airline services since it would take at least three connections to get to Rochester. There were so many kindnesses from so many people that it was a huge help to me during that difficult time.

The last few days before we left are now something of a blur. I had so many things to do. We had to make a will, the solicitor came into the hospital to see Brian. We had to make arrangements for Anita at school and like any other mother, I was fussing around the place trying to leave the freezer full for the boys who were staying at home. The days never seemed to be long enough, every day brought a new list of things to be done. I was like a robot going around getting all the ends tied up. I still didn't appreciate just how ill Brian was and I think I was in a state of shock.

The doctors were anxious to get him to Mayo as soon as possible because they knew that once he arrived there he would have a very rigorous period of testing. They felt he was failing, and his diabetes was very hard to stabilize. So while it was no surprise it was still a shock to be told one morning when I arrived at the Mater, that we would be leaving for Mayo in three days time.

Our doctors had strongly advised us to keep our departure as quiet as possible, since they felt that if it became public knowledge too many people, though well meaning could turn it into a circus which Brian would not be able for. So it was only when I arrived up to his third floor room, that the staff became aware that our departure was imminent. This came as a big shock to them, they had given Brian such wonderful care there, it was not only the superb nursing, but the true kindness we both encountered. They were very fond of Brian and were genuinely upset to see him go. Before we left, the Taoiseach phoned to wish us well on our journey and in America. Brian was very feeble and weak that morning, but he was incredibly aware mentally and he tried to have a word for everyone. He too was upset to be leaving the Mater, but of course, he made every attempt to hide this.

At the airport were the Secretary of the Department of Foreign Affairs, Noel Dorr, Brian's private secretary, Orla O' Hanrahan, press secretary Dick O' Brien and the Taoiseach's personal secretaries Catherine Butler and Eileen Foy. They were kindness itself especially with their gifts of magazines and flowers which helped us on our way. Ready to join for the journey were Gabriel Burke and the medical team of Dr. John Lennon, Dr. Dick Firth and Nurse Bridie Smyth.

CHAPTER SIX

I'll never forget the morning we flew out from Ireland. It had all happened so quickly in the end and there was so much to be done prior to our departure that I really didn't have too much time to think about the enormity of our situation. I stayed at the hospital, quite late, that last night. The children all came in to say their goodbyes then and by complete coincidence I had a call from Brian's only brother Paddy that afternoon, to say that he was in town and if it would be alright for him to visit the hospital. Paddy lives in Athlone on the family farm and we only see him a few times a year, so it was fate that he called that day, because we had decided not even to tell our relations when we were leaving.

Paddy and Brian had a long chat that evening, about family and the old times in Athlone and Brian seemed bright enough when we left. It was well after midnight by the time I got home and started my packing. As I looked into the wardrobe, it suddenly dawned on me that I had no idea how long we were going for. The Mayo Clinic had told us that everything depended on whether Brian would be accepted for a transplant. If not, he would commence a suitable course of treatment. So at that point, it could have been anything from six weeks to six months in America. My mind was spinning as I threw everything into a couple of suitcases. Then I packed some things for Brian too. The hardest part was leaving the children. Poor Anita was due to sit her Intermediate Certificate within a few weeks and I was worried about how she would cope, knowing her Dad was so ill in America. I had arranged with the nuns in Mount Sackville to accept her as a boarder for the duration of our absence. Paul was doing his fifth year at Belvedere and Niall, who was preparing for his Law finals in Trinity, assured me that he would be able to keep an eye on everything at home for me. They were all so brave, which was an enormous boost for me.

Gabriel Burke.

Orla O' Hanrahan.

Dick O' Brien.

Noel Dorr.

Peg Fogarty.

Gerry Staunton.

Since the younger ones were not coming to the airport to see us off, they headed off to school at the usual time that morning. As Anita was going out the door, I started to get a bit weepy. Being the two girls in an otherwise all-male household, I like to think we are very close and the best of pals and I knew that I would miss her greatly in Rochester. I was amazed when she turned to me and said, " Keep your chin up, Mum, and don't let anything get to you and everything will be alright." I couldn't get over the bravery of my fifteen-year-old daughter. Niall drove with me directly to the Mater, where the nurses were already in the process of getting Brian ready for the thirteen-hour flight. There we met Mary O' Rourke who just called to see Brian that morning. The only bit of light relief that I can remember about that morning was when Niall and I said our goodbyes. He has a great sense of fun and his advice for me was, " Now Ma, you'll be able to get a face-lift at the Mayo Clinic." I could only laugh at him.

It seemed quite unreal as we boarded the private jet that would carry us to the world famous clinic that would decide our future. I suppose our time in Foreign Affairs was a huge help because we were used to flying off at a moment's notice. At that stage, I was so tired I could only feel relief that we were finally on our way. I will always say the Mater had done everything humanly possible, way above and beyond the call of duty for both of us. It was their decision that at this stage of his illness, only the Mayo Clinic could help Brian. We had been told about a liver transplant unit in England which also does great work, but this had been ruled out for us on security grounds. So on the one hand I was glad that we were on our way to America because we were all so aware that time was running out for Brian. Indeed Dr. Lennon even seemed apprehensive about the toll the very long journey might have on Brian's very precarious state of health. On the other hand, leaving Ireland was a huge wrench, I knew that this trip was our last resort.

Once we were all aboard, the jet taxied out onto the runway. We were chatting and making small talk because I think the others were acutely aware of just how poignant the departure was for us. I'll never forget the moment we took off from Dublin airport. I looked down on the green fields and over the city. Everything looked so good to me. All I could do was wonder. I wondered about when we would be back home with the family again, I wondered if we would ever come back together and I wondered what the future held in store for us at the world-famous Mayo Clinic. I can honestly say it was the saddest day of my life. The flight was very pleasant. Indeed I thought it was a bit eerie, because once airborne, Brian proceeded to take out his papers and notes to read them as if this was just another working trip. We were able to extend some seats to form a bed and after an hour or so he went for a rest and slept for a few hours. I was very aware of how careful the doctors were to check his sugar levels and his blood pressure throughout the trip. We had a rather nice lunch and of course the never-ending cups of tea and between reading and chatting, the long journey didn't seem like the endurance test we had all been expecting. It was late in the evening when we finally touched down in Rochester. As we made our approach to the airport I remarked to the others how Irish the countryside looked. Masses of rich agricultural countryside as far as the eye could see.

But then this is prairie country, the Mid-West of America, that boasts rolling plains that seem to go on for ever. Once inside the airport you are immediately aware that the Mayo Clinic patients make up the biggest part of the passengers here. Everything in this airport is geared to people who are seriously ill or invalided. Private ambulance jets fly people here not only from all over the States, but from all over the world. At every entrance there were wheelchairs and hospital beds waiting to ferry the incoming people into the Clinic. Two cars from the hospital met us and whisked us quickly into Rochester. Too soon we arrived at the Methodist Hospital where a team of doctors and nurses was waiting for him. Brian was immediately admitted to a room on the fifth floor, while Dr. Rolland Dickson, administrator of the transplant unit was there to meet the Mater team and myself. So while Doctors Lennon and Firth met with their Mayo counterparts to hand over the heavy files of Brian's medical notes, Gabriel and I went over and checked into the Kahler Hotel across the street where we met Ambassador Patrick Mc Kernan who had flown in from Washington to meet us.

After we had thrown our things into our rooms we went back across the street, the ambassador with us, to see Brian settled into his room. Considering everything, he was in very good form. He was very relieved to be finally there and he had great faith in what they would do for him. He was always optimistic about the future, even then when he was quite worn out. I kissed him good-night and then I went to join Dr. Lennon and Dr. Firth who were having dinner with some of the Mayo doctors. I know I must have been exhausted, because I remember very little about the chat that evening. We finished about 1.00a.m. which was 8.00a.m. Irish time. We had been on the go for over twenty-six hours. The real heroes were the two doctors and Bridie Smyth. They left, almost immediately to make the return trip to Ireland. We walked the short journey back to the hotel lobby, where we said our goodbyes. That was a particularly emotional time for me because I felt that as long as I was with the Mater team, I still had a link with Ireland. With their imminent return home, I felt totally alone in this strange city, all links with our Irish medical friends now severed. But they were so reassuring about Brian and they told me to try not to worry. We were in the best place in the world to care for him.

I went up to my 10th floor room. This was to be my home for the foreseeable future. It seemed strange then because I hadn't got used to anything about the place at that point. I looked out the window and I was delighted to be able to see Brian's room across the street. That made me feel nearer to him. But I still felt incredibly lonely. All I knew that night was that I was seven thousand miles away from home, Brian was across the street in hospital and while I had heard of the Mayo Clinic, I never in my wildest dreams thought that we would end up here. I didn't know if he would live or die. Would he be a suitable case for a transplant that could save his life ? After all he was 58 years of age and we knew that Mayo rarely performed liver transplants on patients over 50. I knew how badly he wanted that transplant himself, though I have to admit, I still felt disturbed at the prospect. I twisted and turned in bed. I never felt as lonely in my life before. But then and there I made a pact with myself. There would be no time for tears here. If I couldn't sleep, I would read.

For Brian's sake I had to keep going. Neither of us knew what lay ahead from one day to the next. So I would continue to put my trust in God, continue to say my prayers and take one day at a time. Images were flying through my mind. The happy times with the children growing up, the ups and downs of life in politics, the friends who had been so good to us always and I thought about Brian's mother who had died just a short few months before. She worried so much about him I wondered what she would have made of this last resort journey to the Mayo Clinic. Too bad that she wasn't still with us because we would need all the prayers we could get from now on. And for some strange reason, I thought of Christmas too that night. Would we ever have another family Christmas at home with our relations and neighbours ? While I was unaware then that much tougher times lay ahead for us, looking back now, I have to say that my first night alone in Rochester was the loneliest of the entire time away from home.

CHAPTER SEVEN

Like most people in this country I only knew of the great reputation of the Mayo Clinic when it hit the international headlines, through either some breakthrough in medical science and technology or because some head of state or celebrity was being treated there. Ronald Reagan's laser surgery at St. Mary's Hospital last year grabbed international headlines for over a week, while Barbara Bush's recent thyroid treatment at the Clinic, where I'm delighted to say that she was attended by its top endocrinologist, Irish born, Colum Gorman, was widely covered by the media in America.

But it would be totally wrong to conclude from the patients who have been treated there, though the list reads like an international Who's Who, that the Mayo Clinic cares only for the rich and famous. Nothing could be further from the reality of the day to day running of this vast complex that virtually encompasses the whole town of Rochester. The biggest percentage of Mayo patients are still the farming families from throughout the state of Minnesota. In fact, it is the policy of the Clinic never to turn anyone away who comes there to seek help. However, it is true that people come not only from all over the United States but from all over the world in search of " a Mayo Miracle." When we arrived in search of our Mayo Miracle I knew little or nothing about the philosophy of the Mayo family, the founding fathers of the clinic, which continues to be the guiding force there. I knew nothing about the town of Rochester, where the vast clinic, and hospital complex is located.

Yet, it would be virtually impossible for anyone to stay in the town for any length of time without discovering the origins of the famous Mayo name, because the people of Rochester take such a great pride in the heritage in their midst. Mayo Clinic, a model for medical practice throughout the world, took root and grew in the farm fields near Rochester in Minnesota. It grew from the medical practice of a frontier doctor, William Worral Mayo, an Englishman who migrated to America in 1845 and settled in Rochester in 1863. His sons, William J. Mayo and Charles H. Mayo - known affectionately as Dr. Will and Dr. Charlie joined him in practice in the 1880s. This was the beginning of the era of aseptic surgery and the Mayo brothers became proficient in the new technique. The Mayos continued to add innovative ideas to the country practice. Their tireless work in learning new techniques and creating their own attracted international attention and produced an enviable success rate. The Mayo reputation flourished. Physicians and scientists came from across the nation and around the world to watch the Mayo brothers perform surgery. The family practice grew until it outgrew the family. This dilemma produced the first private group practice of medicine in the world.

The world famous Mayo Clinic.

As the Mayos expanded their practice, they asked other doctors to join them. Specialists in many fields complemented their medical skills. They formed teams of experts, organized so that they could interact and support each other, yet remain dedicated to patient care. The rapid growth of their group practice created the need for a new organization. This system would coordinate the activities of physicians and patients, the training of medical specialists and the growth of medical research. This system became known as the Mayo Clinic. The Mayo brothers died in 1939. Since that time, Mayo Clinic has continued to be guided by their principles and ideals and exists for these purposes: To offer comprehensive medical care of the highest standard; to offer outstanding people opportunities for medical education; to advance knowledge and skill in medicine through medical research. The resources of the Mayo Foundation are used only to achieve these purposes in keeping with the highest moral, ethical and legal standards.

Today the Mayo Clinic story reads like a history of modern medicine. Its chapters include development of new cures, breakthroughs in new procedures and success in new forms of treatment. Mayo and its affiliated hospitals, Rochester Methodist Hospital with over 800 beds and St. Mary's Hospital, one of the biggest in the country with over 1,000 beds, combine to form Mayo Medical Centre, a medical community of 15,000 employees who care for more than 4,000 patients every working day. The medical experts apply the knowledge and skills of many to the needs of each individual patient. It's a medical community focused on patient care, organized so that doctors can spend their time helping patients without worrying about scheduling appointments, locating records or handling administrative details. The result is a team of medical experts focused on the needs of individual patients and inspired by continuous involvement in education and research.

It took me quite some time to find my way to all the different buildings that form the complex. But I was very soon aware that

Rochester and the Mayo Clinic are virtually synonymous. The town's population hovers around 60,000. Over 20,000 are employed in some form of medical or paramedical activity. Since its geographical location in the northern part of the Mid-West dictates sub-zero temperatures in winter as the icy winds blow down from Canada, the town has been organized to operate without ever having to go out of doors.

St. Mary's Hospital, the largest private hospital in the world.

I was unaware that most people who visit the Clinic stay in the various hotels in the town and attend the Clinic daily on an outpatient basis. Only those who are critically ill are admitted to one of the two hospitals. So you have a rather strange situation where most of the guests in the hotels are actually patients at the Clinic. Everything, everywhere is geared to make the patient's life in Rochester easier. Particularly in the hotels, where private nursing can be supplied if required, medication can be delivered as part of room service from the well stocked pharmacy in the lobby, and special dietary requirements never present the slightest problem.

As I said, it's possible to go from most hotels to either the Clinic or hospitals without ever going out of doors. A labyrinth of underground passages provides not only easy access, I was able to take the elevator from outside my bedroom door to the underground walkway that brought me to another elevator which left me right outside Brian's room in the hospital, but I never needed to worry about the weather since in summer these walkways are air-conditioned and in winter they are well heated. These underground walkways also contain a maze of shops. You can find everything from hairdressers and beauty salons, to boutiques, newsstands, luggage stores, shoe repair, even an antique store. Needless to mention there are stores supplying every conceivable type of medical and paramedical supplies as well as a number of extremely well stocked pharmacies and several restaurants. I can tell you, underground at Grand Central Station in New York was never as bustling and alive as the underground in Rochester. And for those who didn't want to be totally isolated underground,

Rochester Methodist Hospital.

there is also an extensive sky walk, an intercommunicating system, which also connects many of the hotels and hospitals over ground.

It took me a while to get used to the fact that there were always wheelchairs in the hotel lobby and at the elevator entrances throughout the buildings. But the system was simple to say the least. If you needed a wheelchair, you picked one up as you might a supermarket trolley, in your hotel, or wherever, and you dropped it off wherever you were going. Then when you were returning, you simply picked up another one. This was much easier than trying to identify your own wheelchair at the Clinic where thousands would be in use each day.

Kahler Hotel.

The pace of life in Rochester is not unlike that of a small Irish town. Everything revolves around the Clinic and hospitals and those who are employed by the Mayos or hotels are usually farming folk. The friendliness of everyone everywhere was one of the first things I noticed about Rochester. In shops and cafés in the town it is automatically assumed that you are visiting for medical reasons, so I became used to the usual greeting of " Hi, where are you from and what are you here for?" Everyone I met either had a medical problem, some more serious than ours, or like myself was accompanying a family member who was hospitalized. I met people from all over the United States as well as many from other parts of the world and it was extremely heartening for me to hear all the praise that everyone seemed to lavish on the different medical teams. No matter how ill or unpleasant the treatment seemed to be, everyone I met had 100% confidence in the Mayo system. It was reassuring for me to hear so many people that I met in the early days at Mayo repeatedly tell me that Brian couldn't get better medical care anywhere.

At the Mayo Clinic.

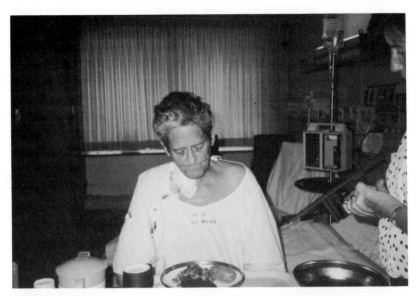

At the Mayo Clinic.

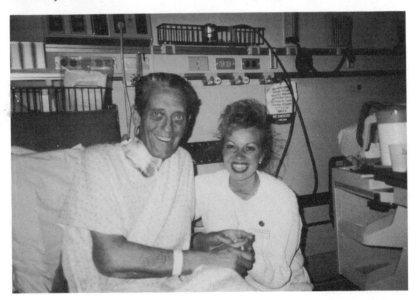

At the Mayo Clinic.

CHAPTER EIGHT

It is part of the Mayo philosophy to provide both the patient and family with as much detailed information as possible about the patient's illness and the treatment he/she will receive in the hospital or at the Clinic. So on my first morning in Rochester, after a sleepless night, I met Dr. Rolland Dickson, administrator of the Liver Transplant Unit, who gave me a comprehensive tour of the 11th floor special liver unit.

As we made our way through space-age operating theatres, Dr. Dickson told me about the origins of liver transplants in the United States and how the Mayo Unit was set up in 1985. The first successful liver transplant was performed by Dr. Thomas Starzl at the University of Colorado, Denver, in 1967. Initial liver transplant operations failed to provide long term survival. Even with major improvements in the surgical technique, one-year survival rates hovered around 20% to 40%. A major turning-point came with the development of the immuno-suppressive (anti-rejection) drug cyclosporine in about 1980. The drug is largely responsible for a two-fold improvement in the one-year liver transplant survival rate from the pre-cyclosporine era.

Cyclosporine was developed by Sandoz Pharmaceuticals of New Jersey in their Switzerland headquarters, following the discovery of an unusual fungus dug up by a vacationing scientist in Hardanger, Norway in 1970. The drug developed from this fungus contains an amino acid yet to be found in any other life form. The drug was approved by the Food and Drug Administration in September 1983 and marketed under the name of Sandimmune.

Dr. Dickson also told me how candidates for transplant are chosen. They suffer from a chronic, progressive liver disease for which no other effective medical or surgical therapy exists. Prospective transplant recipients are first reviewed by a committee of medical and non-medical professionals headed by the transplant surgeon Dr. Ruud Krom. When considering a patient for liver transplant the committee looks primarily at the patient's condition. Another consideration is the patient's quality of life, the extent to which the patient's symptoms are affecting his or her life. Another factor is the patient's willingness and ability to comply with medical therapies required of patients post-operatively, such as taking immuno-suppressive drugs for life. Age is another factor. At Mayo, liver transplants are rarely given to anyone over 50. Brian and I were already aware of this and of course it placed a bigger burden on Brian to convince everyone that at 58 he was still a suitable candidate. The two main conditions that exclude a patient from receiving a liver transplant are active infection and advanced heart or lung disease.

Dr. Rolland Dickson, head of the Liver Transplant Unit.

The Mayo Liver Unit, is already established as one of the largest referral centres for chronic liver disease in the world. Mayo began its liver transplant programme under the direction of Dr. Ruud Krom in January 1985. Twenty-seven months later the 100th liver transplant was performed at Mayo.

When Dr. Krom arrived at Mayo from the Netherlands in 1985, he commented that liver transplant surgery was " no one-man show." The list of specialists integral to the program under-scores his comment. Besides transplant surgeons, the team includes specialists in hepatology (liver), anaesthesiology, inten-sive care medicine, infectious diseases, blood banking, liver pathology, haematology, radiology, nephrology, neurology, virol-ogy and immunology. Paraprofessionals also play important roles. These include the four liver transplant procurement co-ordina-tors, nursing co-ordinators, nurses from the Methodist hospital patient care areas on the 11th and 5th floors, social workers, transplant laboratory specialists, a nutritionist, a chaplain, statis-tics and data specialists and administrative and business office personnel.

As Dr. Dickson showed me around the space-age operating theatre, with its own recovery rooms and intensive care unit, with monitors and machines everywhere and a computer constantly providing the latest data on the patients, I felt quite bewildered. As we made our way through the unit, I knew that I was on trial myself. Mayo made it very clear that in addition to the patient being able to cope with the physical and psychological realities of a transplant, it was vital that spouses, partners or close family members should feel equally confident and comfortable with the transplant and be able to provide real moral and psychological support during the pre-operative treatment as well as during the long post-op. period. And I felt my reaction to everything I saw that day and the way I accepted the information was undoubtedly part of my test.

I had very mixed reactions to what I saw and heard. While I had no doubt that the facilities were the best in the world, I found the

Dr. Rudd Krom, liver transplant surgeon.

high tech. environment intimidating. To me it looked more like Cape Canavaral and I found it hard to think that my Brian might soon be faced with such radical surgery in these surroundings. It all seemed too much for me that day. I know that I was still very tired after the long journey the previous day, but after the Mater this seemed such a major culture shock for me. But I was only too well aware that it was exactly because of these world class facilities that we had made the journey here in the first place. I was equally well aware that Brian might not even be accepted as a transplant candidate. Even at that 11th hour, I was still hoping that his doctors would recommend treatment, I still didn't feel comfortable myself with the concept of a transplant. Basically I was totally in awe of and scared by the prospect of an operation that I still thought of in terms of science fiction.

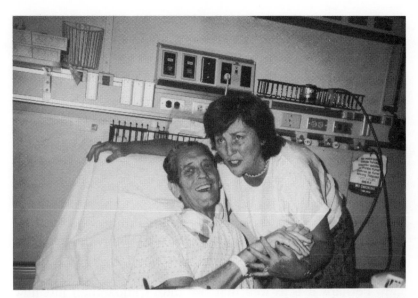

Fighting the battle together.

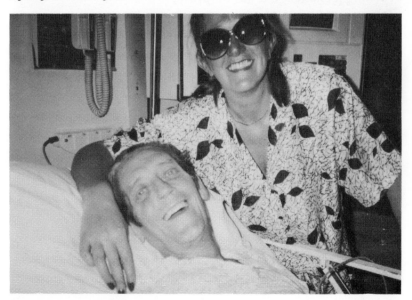

Keeping the spirits up with Gabriel Burke.

On the 3rd floor I discovered a beautiful little non-denominational chapel. After the sci-fi like environment of the 11th floor, this seemed like a veritable oasis of tranquillity. I stayed to say a quick prayer and to collect my thoughts and while I was there I was impressed by the way patients wandered in and out. Some were able to walk on their own, others were wheeled in chairs and even a bed. But they all seemed so positive and even at that very early stage, it gave me a very positive feeling about the hospital too.

When I went down to see Brian in his room on the 5th floor later that morning, he was determined to prove himself a suitable case for a transplant. Although he was very weak after the journey, he had enjoyed a good night's rest and the nurses had already begun to start building him up for the gruelling schedule of at least ten days of tests that lay ahead of him. Brian always loved to rise to a challenge and this would be the ultimate challenge for him. Perhaps it is as well that we didn't know then just how gruelling a challenge it was to prove.

CHAPTER NINE

Within a few days the whole place looked less formidable and insofar as it was possible I settled into my new environment as well as I could. I had come to grips with my immediate surroundings, though I could still get lost if I took the underground subway to visit Brian. Most times, I simply left the hotel by the side-door and crossed the street to the hospital. I developed a routine which made each day seem as normal as possible. I got up about eight each morning and went to the rooftop swimming pool for my daily laps. I felt that the lack of exercise for the past few months was beginning to take its toll. Brian and I loved to take long walks in Phoenix Park or in the country but it had been almost a year since we had enjoyed our strolls with any regularity. Now the proximity of this lovely pool afforded me an ideal way to start the day.

Back in my room, I would get ready for the day. Sometimes I might give Brian a call to see how he was feeling, or what his schedule of tests was for the day. I had a direct line from my room to his and to the nursing station, all of which was very reassuring. Gabriel and I had breakfast in the Coffee Shop in the hotel most mornings about nine. We both liked it there because the staff were so friendly and so cheerful. We also both loved the freshly-baked muffins that were available there. In fact my abiding memory of not only the Kahler Hotel, but of everywhere in Rochester is of just how cheerful and optimistic everyone was all the time. Of course as I said earlier, everything in Rochester revolves around the Mayo Clinic, even the hotel we stayed in is partly owned by the hospital.

After breakfast I would go over to see Brian while Gabriel went back to her room to start her day's work on the 'phone and fax to Foreign Affairs in Dublin, the Embassy in Washington or the Consulate in Chicago. The high point of the day for us was when she returned with all the news from home. She usually brought

Recuperating.

With some of the Liver Transplant Team.

stacks of letters and Mass cards from well-wishers all over Ireland. Many came from friends and constituents, but we also received numerous good wishes from complete strangers. I have to say that this was very heartening for us. I didn't feel quite so alone in America knowing we had so much goodwill, support and prayers coming from home. I felt that if prayers could cure Brian, then he definitely had a head start. He was very determined to prove himself during the ten days of testing. He knew that his first important battle was to convince the doctors that he was a suitable case for a transplant. The tests were going well for him, but he had some really gruelling days. I remember one day he was gone from early in the morning until late in the evening undergoing an arduous kidney test. He was quite worn out when he came back to his room after that one. He looked frail and drawn and I wondered just how much stamina he had left to cope with the days ahead. But after a good night, he bounced back the next day and was in good form again.

In the evenings, Gabriel and I would have dinner in one of the restaurants near the hotel. It was nice to get away from the hotel for a break. Afterwards we would go back to see Brian. Sometimes we would rent a video. They had a video library in the hospital, which I thought was such a good idea, and that would pass a couple of hours for us. Of course with the news channels like CNN on the television, Brian was never short of something to watch. He read a lot during those days, he was determined to be rested and in as tip-top shape as possible for the doctors. There were a number of Irish consultants at the Mayo Clinic and they were kindness itself. In the early days they 'phoned to say hello and to assure me that if we needed anything during our stay, that they would be delighted to help out. I wasn't really able to accept all their invitations at the beginning because I wanted to spend as much time as I could with Brian. But on my first Sunday there, Colum Gorman, who is one of the leading endocrinologists in the United States, and his wife Una invited me to their home. First they took me to Mass at St. Brigid's Church, a lovely little Irish church about fifteen minutes outside Rochester. It was set on a hill and surrounded by very fertile farming land. I immediately thought that it could have been in Tipperary or somewhere else in Ireland. We went into the graveyard after Mass and it was fascinating to see all the Irish names on the headstones. Dating from the middle of the last century, the church was set up for the Irish who had emigrated all the way out to this part of the Mid-West. What a long trek it must have been to go so far off the beaten track, because it wasn't an obvious place for the Irish to settle in the United States.

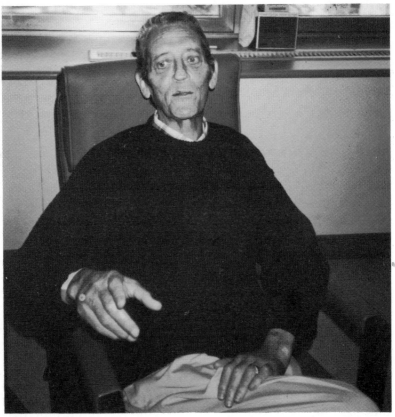

Making a point.

Celebrating with Jack's army.

4

With Speaker Foley, September 1988.

With Prime Minister Papandreou of Greece, President of the E.C. - Rhodes Summit, December 1988.

At the White House with Ronald Reagan and Margaret Heckler.

Addressing the United States Congress.

Reviewing the guard of honour in Athens.

Foreign Ministers meeting in Copenhagen.

Arriving at the Vatican.

With His Holiness, Pope John Paul II.

Official visit to Canada 1989.

With Brian and Mila Mulroney.

The Mayo Clinic, the world's largest medical practice.

Part of the Mayo Clinic art collection.

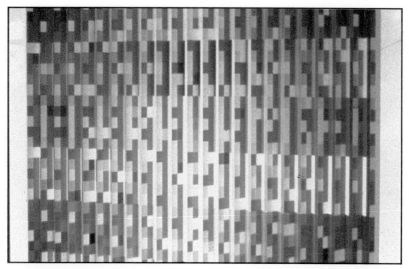

The revolving kaleidescope of colour, appropriately titled "Welcome", stands in the lobby of the Clinic.

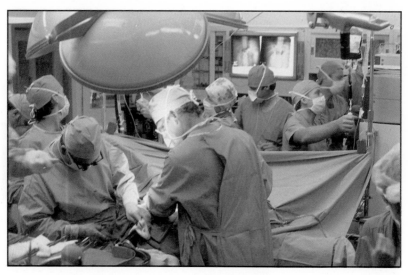

A liver transplant operation in progress at the Mayo Clinic.

St Mary's Hospital, the largest private hospital in the United States.

The Rochester Methodist Hospital.

Winging our way home, June 1989.

First day back at Leinster House.

Glad to be back, Rochester, January 1990.

Dublin can be heaven … with a stroll in Stephen's Green.

After Mass we went to the Gormans' home in the suburbs where we had a real American brunch, which was something we hadn't had before in a private house. We met quite a few of the Irish doctors there - Michael Brennan from Dublin and his wife Rebecca, Brendan Moore, also from Dublin, who was a liver specialist, and his wife Mary from Kilkenny. There also were Michael and Margaret Sullivan from Listowel and Dan and Ruth Connolly. Dan, now semi-retired, is one of the most senior of the Irish doctors at Mayo and is a great friend of President Hillery. And we met Des O'Duffy and his wife Terry from Tipperary on that occasion too. They were all very kind and caring and I appreciated the fact that they weren't intrusive asking questions about Brian. Of course they would pop into the hospital to see him. They would just put their heads around the door and stay for a minute or two. They knew he wasn't able for visitors at that stage. Most of them had emigrated there in the Sixties and have made very good lives for themselves. Quite a few of them come back to Ireland for holidays regularly and they were all keen to hear about the news from home. They were particularly interested to hear about the EEC and how it was affecting Ireland. All in all it was a very pleasant afternoon. A nice breakaway from the routine. They drove us back to the hospital and we went to tell Brian all the news of our day out. He was delighted that we had enjoyed ourselves so much.

As the days progressed, the transplant became the whole focus of our lives. Everything revolved around those tests. We met some counsellors and social workers from the Liver Transplant Team. Every Tuesday and Friday there were counselling sessions which about twenty people would attend and to which we were invited. Some, like ourselves, were still waiting to be accepted for the operation, while others were already on the waiting list. Everyone had their own story to tell. It was comforting to hear other people's problems and to know that ours were often same. That gave me a bit of confidence. Because I used to worry so much about all of the tests and their effects, it was great to realise that others were in exactly the same situation. It was indeed a case of a problem

Enjoying a chat with Jane.

Relaxing with Gabriel.

shared. But what gave me the greatest hope was the number of post-transplant patients who attended. You really wouldn't believe that they had been ill at all. In fact I often said to Gabriel that many of the family support groups like ourselves looked worse than those recovering from the operation. We all looked rather tired and worn out. I felt if such an amazing improvement could be brought about by the transplant, then there was hope that Brian's life could return to normal again too. It was also fascinating to listen to others in that group, who would be back in the Clinic for their annual check-up. They were so positive about their lives and the new quality of life the operation had given them, that we felt that Brian could not be accepted for the operation soon enough.

I could only wonder at the thoroughness of the testing to which Brian continued to be subjected, particularly his main organs, heart, lungs and kidneys. Now the fact that he had never smoked became a major plus factor and also the fact that he had been extremely active all his life from his soccer days in UCD. On our tenth day at Mayo, we received the news that was literally music to our ears. Brian was finally accepted as a transplant patient and his name had been activated on the United Network for Organ Sharing, a computer system that matches donated organs with waiting patients throughout the United States. For liver patients, size of body, blood type and nearness to death are among the data keyed into the computer. The doctors subsequently told us that the fact that his main organs were in such good condition was a decisive factor in his being accepted for the transplant operation.

Brian was given a bleeper which allowed us to travel within twenty miles of Rochester and I could hardly contain myself when he was discharged to join me across the street at the Kahler Hotel.

We knew that on any given day roughly 500 Americans are awaiting liver transplants. But the supply of available livers rarely exceeds four or five, so transplant centres have to compete fiercely for the scarce organs. We also knew that Brian's opportunity for a new life totally depended on somebody else losing theirs. I think that I found that whole issue the hardest of all, because we knew it was Mayo policy never to reveal the identity of the donor and that we would never be able to meet the donor's family to thank them for their great generosity to us. How do you thank someone for giving you the greatest gift of all, the gift of a new life ?

Now the real waiting had begun.

A lovely day out with Brendan and Mary Moore and their daughter, Anna.

CHAPTER TEN

As we settled into a new routine, I couldn't believe the difference having Brian back with me made to our day-to-day living. Our hotel room was transformed by his presence and now it really was a home from home for us. The General Manager, Kevin Molloy from Dublin and his wife Cinta from Co. Mayo went out of their way to make our stay as comfortable as possible and we really didn't want for anything. Brian loved to get the papers early in the morning and of course Gabriel had the daily bulletins that came out from Foreign Affairs so we had a good idea of what was happening at home. We kept in touch with the family with frequent 'phone calls and it was a big load off my mind that they all seemed to be getting on quite well in our absence. My brother Conor kept in touch with us all the time. He promised me that the minute Brian went in for his operation that he and Clic would fly out to join me. Right now there was no point in having them fly out while we were waiting, because we had no idea how long that wait would be. We knew that some patients had been waiting for a suitable liver for months, but we tried not to think about that.

Of course Brian still had to go back to the Clinic every second day to have further tests and to be monitored. These were long days when he would get up shortly after six to make his way across the road to the white marble, nineteen-storey clinic which has become a citadel of hope for the terminally ill. Gabriel insisted on getting up and coming with us on those early starts. I appreciated her company because so much time was spent waiting for Brian to come out of one consultant before going in to another one, it was nice to have some company. On the days he was at the Clinic, naturally Brian was exhausted by evening time. Then we had a really quiet time in an attempt to give him as much rest as possible. We even had dinner in our room on those evenings.

On the alternate days when he was free we took it easy too. We went for short walks through the town browsing in the shops and of course we still attended the counselling meetings at the hospital. They kept us in touch with the others in the Liver Unit who, like us were also waiting for a life-saving transplant. There was great camaraderie among the group and at times I found myself almost forgetting just what tied us all together. On those days we would take lunch in NED's cafeteria in the first floor of the hospital. This pleasant mini coffee shop served breakfast, lunch and dinner as well as in-between snacks and all the food was planned by the resident dietician. So, since Brian was still on a carefully planned diet it was easy for all of us to eat here where we knew the food was suitable for him. It was also helpful for us to learn how to cope with practical aspects of following a diet when we would eventually return home.

We encouraged him to join us for short trips out into the adjoining countryside. It was really beautiful around Rochester and since we had never been to that part of the Mid -West before, it was a real treat to have time to do some sightseeing. It was a most welcome distraction for all of us.

One Sunday afternoon we had a very pleasant outing to Michael and Rebecca Brennan's home. We had a great chat, sitting outside in the garden in the sunshine. It was great to hear all the news from home. Brian was in fine form that afternoon. Another time we took a trip out to the historic village of Mantorville. From our hotel it was only a twenty minute drive on Highway 14, but that small distance actually spans a century. Listed in the National Register of Historic Places, this village looks much the same now as it did in the nineteenth century, which is only natural since many of its buildings and homes date from the 1860s and have been preserved perfectly. A village of five hundred inhabitants, whose fame, like Rochester's, seems far out of proportion to its size, Mantorville is the seat of Dodge County and its courthouse has been in continuous use since 1865. Here too we saw Hubbell

Time stands still in Mantorville.

House, one of Minnesota's oldest and most famous restaurants which was once an inn for the stage coaches carrying pioneers out to the Wild West. We saw the Opera House which dates from 1918, the Restoration House which remains unchanged since 1856 and of course we couldn't miss the famous boardwalk. Names of early settlers had been engraved into the wooden path and we were fascinated to read a number of Irish names included with the emigrants who seemed to have come from all over Europe, particularly Germany and the Scandinavian countries. There were also many names of people moving from the east coast of America and imagine our surprise when we actually came upon a Lenihan family listed here from all those years ago. We would have loved to have had the time to have followed up on that pioneering branch of the family who were way out West in the mid 1800s. We planned a return trip to the village, but events overtook us and we never did get back there.

Lake Pepin.

On these drives we were really taken with the big barns dotted throughout the countryside which are special to this part of America and the barn-covered bridges were something that we had not seen before elsewhere. This was really Mark Twain countryside and it brought back memories of classics like Huckleberry Finn, which of course we had all read in school. We even got a video of Huckleberry Finn to watch one evening. We all got quite a kick out of identifying the countryside. It seemed hard to think back to those years long ago at school in Athlone, reading the works of Mark Twain, that we would one day find ourselves in the middle of the countryside that was his inspiration.

Another day we went out to legendary Lake Pepin, a widening of the Mississippi which is a fishing haven and sailing spa east of Rochester. It was here that Ralph Samuelson invented the technique of water skiing in 1922. Brian was very quiet that day. I think it was the only occasion during our whole stay in America that he seemed to be down in himself. He was walking along by the lakeshore and he told me it reminded him so much of the lake back home on the Shannon. It brought back memories of his happy childhood in Athlone, where so much of his time was spent out by the lake. He wasn't feeling too well that day and I think he must have been wondering just how long he would have to wait for his operation. At the back of his mind too I think was the worry that if it was much longer that he might not make it to the operation.

After that trip to the Lake he didn't want to go out again. Like many liver patients he was suffering from acites, a swelling of fluid in the stomach that is extremely uncomfortable. As the days passed, this condition got much worse, he almost looked pregnant. With the exceedingly hot and humid weather, it was very weakening for him to try to move about outdoors, so he was happy to stay inside in the air-conditioned room, where he continued his reading. The doctors were monitoring his acites but they were reluctant to bring him back into hospital to drain his stomach. They were fearful that this could well induce infection, which in his present condition he was not strong enough to fight. It was becoming a classic case of Catch 22, because if he had an operation to drain his stomach and infection set in, then should a liver become available for him he would be unable for the transplant. Yet, I could see that the acites was getting worse, his stomach was becoming more and more swollen and that he was now rapidly deteriorating. That was the hardest part of all, the waiting and waiting. We knew that he was not feeling well and it was quite unlike Brian to be feeling down.

The prairies.

On the Saturday of that week, we had Mass said in the little chapel in the hospital. We knew we had much to be thankful for already. That Brian was on the waiting list was indeed good news for us. We knew that he was was 11th on the waiting list, but we had no means of knowing just how long it would take to find a suitable liver. Looking back now, that was one of the hardest parts of our time in Rochester, the fact that you did not have the slightest idea of how long the wait might be. Of course there was nothing that anyone could do to help us, because at the hospital they didn't know until they got word of a suitable organ themselves. Always at the forefront of my mind was the fact that we knew that before Brian got his liver, someone else had to die. I found that very hard to come to grips with, so every night, I prayed and prayed. In our first ten days at the hospital it wasn't an issue since then we didn't know whether he would be accepted for the transplant or not, but once he was accepted I became very apprehensive about everything.

Though we didn't speak about it among ourselves, we knew that the biggest battle still had to be fought.

CHAPTER ELEVEN

We will never forget Tuesday May 23rd. It started off just like any other morning for us. Brian was not due to go to the Clinic that day, so we were getting up a little later than usual. He had left his bleeper on the bedside table the previous evening and we were well rehearsed by the doctors in the procedure if it went off. I was still in bed watching breakfast television, Brian was shaving in the bathroom with the door closed, when suddenly this piercing bleep began to sound. For a minute I didn't know what it was. Suddenly my eyes alighted on the famous bleeper near the bed. Yet I couldn't believe what I was hearing. I became totally numb, I didn't know what to do. He hadn't heard it himself, so I jumped out of bed, threw on my dressing gown and raced out to Gabriel's room down the corridor. Thankfully, she was cool, calm and collected. She came to our room and 'phoned the number we had been given. Dr. Dickson was at the other end and he told us to come over to the hospital immediately. Brian, still in his pyjamas, wanted to know if there was time to get dressed. Dr. Dickson was quite amused at that cool reaction but told him not to bother, since the operating theatre demanded a very different dress code.

However, he managed to put on some clothes over his pyjamas and we set off from the hotel. My own recollections are hazy because I couldn't believe that it was finally happening. But Brian was so calm, you'd nearly think he was going out for a morning stroll. I just couldn't believe the enormity of what lay ahead for him. The next ten hours would decide our future. Would we ever take a stroll together again ? Was Brian strong enough to make it through the massive operation and, even if he was, would it be a success ?

I remembered the way we had checked out the best possible route to the hospital to be ready for just this occasion. We thought that to put Brian in a wheelchair and to push him through the subway and up into the hospital would be the easiest for him. But here we were actually walking out the front door of the hotel, with Gabriel and myself linking him as we made the short journey. It couldn't have taken even five minutes, across the street and into the ground floor of the hospital. We were making small talk and Brian even managed a joke about being so lucky to have two lovely ladies on his arms. My heart was in my mouth, but I knew that Brian would not want an emotional scene at that stage. I have to say that he was quite remarkable. For him it was a job to be done and got over with as soon as possible. So we were all outwardly very calm when we walked out of the lift into the 11th floor where the transplant team was already waiting for us. While everywhere was hustle and bustle with nursing staff flying all over the place, the procedure seemed different to what we had been expecting. We had expected Brian to be notified once a liver became available and then to be admitted to the Special Liver Unit to be prepared for the marathon operation which normally takes anything from ten hours to perform. But we didn't know then that the liver Brian was about to receive had not been harvested for him at all. Another patient who was ahead of him on the waiting list was due to receive it but when they operated on him, they discovered that he had too many complicating factors for a successful transplant. It was just sheer good luck, that this very same liver was a perfect match for Brian.

He was whisked away to be prepared immediately and Dr. Krom came to talk to me with Dr. Dickson. Dr. Krom kept telling me how lucky Brian was to get this opportunity, that it was a very rare incident. Because I was so flustered I thought he was talking about the opportunity to be accepted for a transplant and I couldn't understand why he was making such a point of it at that stage. It wasn't until it was all over that I finally realised how doubly blessed we had been. Within minutes, Brian was wheeled back to the general area on his way to the operating theatre. Dr. Dickson allowed us to wheel him right to the door with himself and Dr. Krom. It seemed totally unreal after all these months that Gabriel and I should be wheeling him ourselves towards the operating theatre. He was as calm as ever. He had always said that if the Lord wanted him to live, then the operation would be a success. And if he didn't, we had to welcome his will on that too.

At the door of the theatre, Brian took off his wedding ring and pressed it into my hand and kissed me. It could have been a difficult parting but Ruud Krom made us all laugh when he said,"C'mon now, Brian, we want to get this over with. Remember, we have a date to play a round of golf in Ireland." We all laughed and suddenly the double doors swung shut in my face and Dr. Dickson took me back down to the little sitting area by reception. It was then I understood about the reason for the great rush to get the operation under way. A harvested liver can only survive seventeen hours outside of the body, and several hours had already been spent on the other patient.

Dr. Dickson advised us to go back to the hotel to wait since there would be absolutely no word for at least four hours. He promised to call us then with the latest news and to keep us posted during the day on how the operation was progressing. Gabriel and I went back to our room and the first thing she did was to order a drink for me. I can tell you we both needed a drink after that start to the day.

I 'phoned the family to tell them that their Dad was actually being operated on and it was another coincidence that my brother Conor was there in the house when I called. He had been in Dublin for a meeting and he decided to call by to hear the latest news from Mayo and to see how the boys were managing for themselves. Conor was as good as his word. Then and there he said that he and Clic would catch a 'plane the following morning to come out here to support us. So that was very good news and something to look forward to.

As the hours passed, I tried to read and I tried to watch television but my concentration was completely gone. At a quarter to three, I left to go over to the hospital for Mass. It seemed so strange for me to be there on the third floor praying for Brian who was at that minute being operated on a few floors above me. I felt totally helpless since there was nothing I could do to affect the outcome of the operation. The priest said special prayers for Brian and for all our family which was a great comfort for me.

When I got back to the hotel, less than an hour later, Gabriel was in a high state of excitement. Dr. Dickson had 'phoned to say that everything was going much better than expected and that the operation had passed the half-way mark. The old liver had been successfully removed - that in itself is a major, extremely precise piece of surgery - and they had set about transplanting the new liver. He felt the operation might well finish early and he suggested that we go back over to the hospital around six that evening. We were both absolutely over the moon. We felt that everything that had happened that day had been a good omen and now there were only a few hours left before we knew the immediate outcome. The time flew by and there we were again making the return trip across the street and up to the 11th floor. This time there was a distinct spring in our step that had not been there earlier in the morning.

Again we waited in the little reception room by the nurses' station and we were watching all the staff flying around the unit. Over sixty people make up the transplant team, so it is a formidable sight to see these professionals in action. They go about their work with such confidence that it's hard to remember that not too long ago this surgical procedure would have been considered almost like science fiction. Suddenly I saw Brian being wheeled passed me at great speed. For a minute my heart stopped because he had tubes coming out of him everywhere and he looked very grey and was attached to a life support. They were in a hurry to transfer him to a special bed in the intensive care unit where he would again be hooked up to everything in that totally controlled environment. While he looked terrible, it was great to see he was alive.

Shortly afterwards they allowed us in to see him. Despite the high tech. surroundings, his station looked like something out of Cape Canavaral, with flashing lights and bleeping monitors and computers spewing out reams of information. He seemed quite comfortable but totally unconscious. The two intensive care nurses who would be minding him all night said it would probably be the early hours of the following morning when he would fully regain consciousness. So we didn't stay very long on that first visit. Going back to the hotel Gabriel and I were so relieved but still extremely anxious. We knew the next forty-eight hours were extremely critical. We were both in tears. It was still hard to come to grips with the fact that not only had Brian's surgery, so far, been a success, but that his doctors were already predicting a speedy recovery. Everything had gone just like a textbook case, Dr. Dickson told us. At no time had there ever been even the slightest complication. It was, he said, one of the most straightforward transplants they had ever done at Mayo. Brian's life-saving liver, Dr. Dickson told me, had been donated by a young man who had been killed the previous evening in a water-skiing accident out at the very lake where days earlier we had taken that nostalgic walk. We would never know his identity and all I could think of was how his family must be grieving for him while we were celebrating Brian's success.

Once I had 'phoned our family to tell them our good news, I suddenly realised how tired I was myself. But I was still feeling quite euphoric. Yes, it was a day none of us will ever forget. Brian had become the 189th liver transplant recipient at the Rochester Hospital and the eight Irish person to receive a new liver.

I can now understand why at Mayo they called it his new birthday.

CHAPTER TWELVE

Since we came home from America, people have often asked me about the transplant operation, and exactly what is involved in the precise life-saving surgery. In fact it is a tale of two teams, the team that goes out to harvest the liver from the donor, which can be anywhere throughout the United States, and the team that performs the transplantation at the Methodist Hospital at Mayo.

One of the first of many fact sheets that we received once Brian had been accepted for a transplant was, 'Liver Transplantation at Mayo Clinic At A Glance'. It made very interesting if not rather daunting reading for us then.

 * The liver is the largest organ in the body - it weighs about three pounds.

* The liver is the body's refinery. It converts food to energy, processes drugs, aids digestion by producing bile and removes toxins from the blood.

* Liver disease is the fourth leading cause of death in the United States up to age sixty-five.

* Liver transplantation was first successfully performed by Dr. Thomas Starzl at the University of Colorado in 1967.

* About thirty-five U.S. medical centres perform liver transplants, with a one year survival rate of 65%

* One year survival rate at Mayo is 85%.

Life is not possible without the liver, the body's largest organ. The liver is located behind the lower ribs on the right-hand side of the abdomen. It weighs about three pounds and is roughly the size of a football. The liver functions as the body's refinery, converting food into usable energy, processing ingested drugs into forms easier for the body to use, producing bile to break down ingested fatty foods, and removing and excreting toxins from the bloodstream.

In the United States, over 50,000 people die from liver disease each year. The effects of chronic liver disease include severe exhaustion, weight loss, intractable itching, bleeding irregularities and bone fracturing. Researchers have noted that liver disease appears to be on the rise. Chemicals, environmental pollutants and the increasing consumption of medicines are thought to be partly responsible. An estimated 4,000 people become candidates for a liver transplant each year in the United States; only six hundred to seven hundred actually become recipients, due in part to a shortage of available organs.

The liver diseases commonly treated with transplantation at Mayo are chronic active hepatitis, primary bilary cirrhosis, primary sclerosing cholangitis and a number of rarer conditions which include haemochromatosis. Candidates for liver transplantation suffer from a chronic progressive liver disease for which no other effective medical or surgical therapy exists. Prospective transplant recipients are first reviewed by a committee of medical and non-medical professionals headed by Ruud Krom, the transplant surgeon. When considering a patient for liver transplant the committee looks primarily at the patient's condition. Another condition is the patient's quality of life, the extent to which the patient's symptoms are affecting his or her life. Another factor is the patient's willingness and ability to comply with medical therapies required of patients post-operatively, such as taking immunosuppressive drugs for life.

There are essentially only two conditions which would exclude a patient from receiving a liver transplant: active infection and advanced heart or lung disease. The many complications of advanced liver disease may ultimately make transplant surgery too risky for the patient. These factors are weighed by the surgeon and the patient when considering a liver transplant.

From the moment one of Mayo's four organ procurement co-ordinators receives word that a donor liver is available, a cascade of events taking as long as twelve hours (depending on how far the procurement team must travel) occurs before the liver arrives at Mayo. Because illnesses may compromise the health or function of a donated organ, donor organs are obtained primarily from people who die from trauma to the head, or cerebral bleeding. Once brain death is determined and consent is given by the family for organ donation, the patient's blood type and body size and weight are matched to the prospective recipient through a sophisticated system called the United Network of Organ Sharing (UNOS).

If the organ is determined to be acceptable by a Mayo transplant surgeon, an organ procurement team will fly to the donor site to remove the liver in a three- to four-hour operation. Almost all potential liver donors are considered for multiple organ donation, including the heart, pancreas, lungs and kidneys. Once the donor liver is removed, it is infused with a preservative solution and placed in an ice-filled, insulated container for transport. Time is of the essence, which in turn determines the distance Mayo's procurement team can travel to obtain an organ. Livers remain undamaged for about seventeen hours from the time they are harvested.

Once the donor liver is decided to be acceptable, the prospective transplant is notified and surgical support services at Mayo-affiliated Rochester Methodist Hospital are alerted to prepare for the transplant operation. The liver transplant operation begins about one and a half hours before the donor liver arrives in the operating room at the hospital. Surgeons do not remove the prospective recipient's diseased liver until the donor organ is inspected by the transplant surgeons at Methodist Hospital.

The liver is the body's blood cleaning organ and therefore is full of blood vessels. Extensive skill and time of at least eight hours (although complications may extend the operation by several more hours) are required for liver removal and transplantation. The greatest portion of the operation involves removing the diseased liver.

Usually a considerable amount of blood is lost during liver transplant surgery. Blood loss during liver transplants at Mayo averaged about fifteen units through Mayo's first sixty transplants. Special blood salvaging equipment returns about one third of the blood lost back to the patient during surgery. In the initial twenty-four to thirty-six hour period following the operation the patient remains at a Methodist Hospital intensive care unit where he or she is attended by at least one physician from the Transplant Critical Care Service at all times. The patient is also provided with a two-to-one nurse to patient ratio and a one-to-one respiratory therapist to patient ratio. The nurses and the therapist, who receive special training in the care of liver transplant patients, continuously monitor and assess all organ systems and laboratory results and inform the physician of changes in the patient's status.

In the normal course of events, the hospital suggest that patients can expect to stay in the hospital for about four weeks, at the special station on the fifth floor, where post-surgical monitoring, medication teaching and physical therapy occurs. After discharge from the hospital, patients remain in Rochester for about six more weeks at least, or until they are considered in a stable condition. Patients receive twice-weekly check-ups during this time.

As I said earlier, for the prospective liver transplant patient, the burden of catastrophic illness is compounded by financial concerns. The institution where the liver transplantation is performed is also challenged by the high cost of this advanced treatment. At Mayo, the costs of obtaining the donor liver (including transportation of the organ) , the operation, a lengthy hospital stay, extensive laboratory work, blood products and a multitude of possible post-operative complications cannot ethically be passed on to other patients in order to ease the financial burden of liver transplant patients. For this reason, Mayo requires proof of ability to pay the costs of the operation prior to surgery. The average cost of liver transplantation at Mayo varies from $150,000 to $200,000, but can be much higher depending on complications. Most often proof of ability to pay is in the form of a health insurance programme's verification that surgery and subsequent hospitalisation will be paid. In our case the VHI were agreeable to making a contribution towards the cost. But, as I've already said, a group of our friends made up the balance for us.

Mayo Clinic social workers and business office personnel assist every patient in identifying and taking advantage of available financial resources.

While the cost of liver transplantation is indeed staggering, it has been shown that the costs of treating the many complications of liver disease can dwarf the cost of a potentially curative liver transplant.

CHAPTER THIRTEEN

I was awake at the crack of dawn the morning after the operation. For a short time, I couldn't make up my mind whether I had dreamt everything that had happened the previous day. Everything had happened so quickly and so differently to what I had expected. In a way, it had almost been like a 'normal' operation, because everything had gone so smoothly. I kept in touch by 'phone with the Intensive Care Unit during the night. And now with first light, just shortly after six a.m. I called again. The sister in charge told me that he was in good form and had had a very restful night. " Everything is going very smoothly, Mrs. Lenihan, but we must warn you that the first forty-eight hours are critical with transplant patients. If a rejection is likely to occur, there's a high probability that it will happen during that time," she told me.

So while I was relieved to hear that Brian was in good shape, I still felt very apprehensive about the next few days. However, caution went out of my mind when Gabriel and I went across to visit our patient shortly after breakfast. He looked tired, and of course he still had drips coming out of everywhere, but he was amazingly alert and in real fighting form. He was delighted to see us and one of his first questions was when was he going to be allowed a decent steak dinner. After nearly eighteen months on a diet of chicken and fish, Brian who is a real 'meat and potatoes' man, felt that he at least deserved a slap-up meal.

He told us that during the night when he regained consciousness, the two intensive care nurses were there by his bedside. "One was a beautiful blonde from Sweden and the other was an equally striking brunette from Germany. For a minute I thought I was in Heaven", he joked. And even then he was not short of a bit of repartee with the girls. " Hasn't America much to be thankful for to the Old World?" he laughed, still flying the European Flag. In

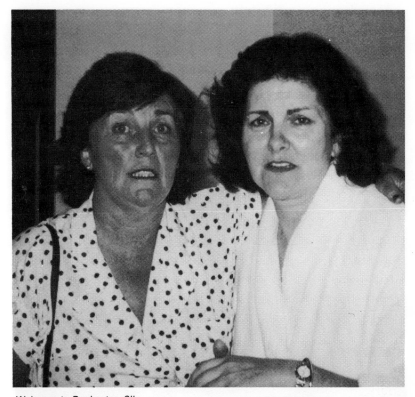

Welcome to Rochester, Clic.

my wildest dreams I had never imagined that he would have been in such great spirits little more than twelve hours after his operation.

So I was in a great state of excitement when Conor and Clic arrived late that night. It had taken them over twenty hours to make the journey from Dublin and it was a very emotional reunion for all of us. They had missed a connection out of London and had to travel, what seemed to be half-way around the world to get to Rochester. It was too late to go over to see Brian then, but even though the travellers were worn out, we still talked late into the night. I was delighted to be able to pass on my great news about

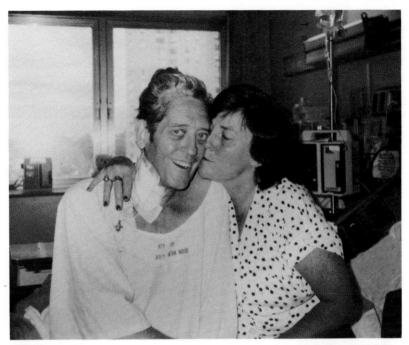

A hug for health.

With Conor Devine.

Brian's amazing recovery and they couldn't wait to see him for themselves the following morning. Of course I was thrilled to hear all the news from home. It was great to hear that Anita and the boys were managing and also to hear the news about our friends and neighbours.

Over dinner, we chatted and at times it was hard to remember that we were actually thousands of miles from home in a strange town, it seemed almost like old times. It was such a relief for Gabriel and myself to have family with us. Suddenly I didn't feel quite as vulnerable or alone as I had been. We talked late into the night. While the two travellers must have been exhausted, they were the last to leave and we arranged to have breakfast together the following morning. We met in the Coffee Shop shortly after 9.30a.m. Conor and Clic were both as fresh as daisies, though they had only had a few hours sleep. After breakfast we made our way across the street to the hospital and took the lift to the 11th floor Intensive Care Unit. We went straight to Brian's station.

When we got there his bed was empty and my heart sank. For one minute my mind was in total turmoil. What had gone wrong? Why hadn't they called me? And I remembered it was still within the critical forty-eight hour period. While it seemed like hours at the time, it must barely have been more than a few seconds before one of Brian's nurses arrived with a big smile on her face. "Didn't anyone tell you, Ann, he was moved back to his own room this morning. He doesn't need us to care for him anymore. He's improving by leaps and bounds from one hour to the next," she said.

We couldn't quite absorb what had happened. Brian had gone from Intensive Care, within twenty-four hours of his operation, when I had been told that he could be there for anything up to a week ! We galloped back to the lift and down to the fifth floor, where we were in for another shock. When we got to his room there was no sign of him, when suddenly the door of the bathroom opened and there was Brian shaving himself. Conor nearly had a fit. Brian was as cool as a breeze - he just laughed and said, " How are things, Conor ?" Conor was nearly speechless but he was quick enough when he finally realised what was going on. " My God Brian, I have patients at home, guys with appendicitis who don't get out of bed for a week and look at you." I think that Conor was more shocked than Brian all of that day. He kept saying what great stamina and strength Brian must have. While I was surprised that events were moving so quickly, Conor, the doctor in our family, was even more surprised than I was.

Here's the beef.

We took some photographs of him that day, he was in such good form. He was particularly pleased with the great big steak that he was given for dinner. "The first decent meal I've had for nearly two years," he joked and we took a special photograph to record that historic moment with Brian giving his steak dinner the thumbs-up sign. We couldn't get over what great form he was in. He was chatting and wanted to know everything that was going on. I thought he was even beginning to look so much better too. That awful yellow colour was gradually disappearing, it was almost like a transformation in front of our eyes. Though I didn't know it at the time, Brian had already been given a certain amount of information about the donor of his new liver. It was general information, sex, age and the cause of death. One of the first things that he did was to write a letter to the donor's mother, thanking herself and her family for the second chance at life her son had given him. The hospital forwarded the letter and Brian received a lovely reply from the boy's mother. I was quite unaware that this correspondence had gone on until much later, but it was something Brian wanted to do as soon as he could.

He was already planning to attend the Friday counselling session the following day and was looking forward to meeting his own group. I think he was secretly very proud of his rapid recovery and knew that it would provide hope for the others who were awaiting their transplants, especially Sally Hauser from Ohio, who had become a good friend. She was expecting her transplant imminently, and at 34, she had the same brave and gutsy attitude

Clic with Martin Burke.

to the operation as Brian. He also planned a special Mass for the following Saturday, the chaplain came and discussed it with him. He wanted it said for the donor and his family and we would all be there. That evening, I was just beginning to relax and finally feel that maybe now there was some light at the end of the long tunnel after all. Brian was improving almost visibly from one hour to the next. Conor and Clic were planning to make this their holiday break and would stay for a few weeks. I felt that by the time they were ready to leave Rochester, Brian should be well on the road to recovery. But there was no rush. I wanted him to take as long as

Catching up with the news.

necessary to make sure that everything was absolutely perfect, before we would even begin to start thinking about coming home. Even the fact that I was thinking along these lines just two days after the operation seemed quite miraculous.

But politics was again about to change the course of our lives. Even out here, we wouldn't be able to escape it. Late on Thursday night Brian Jnr. 'phoned to tell me that the Dáil had been dissolved and a General Election called. "What's Dad going to do, Mum? Will he want to stand? The candidates will be selected next Sunday and Éamon Nolan, Dad's Director of Elections has been bombarded with calls from supporters. Everyone's hoping that Dad will be able to stand," he said. I couldn't believe it when I came off the 'phone. I have to admit that I felt cross that even at this critical time in our lives, politics again became a dominant issue. Later that evening the Taoiseach called to tell me of the election himself. He couldn't have been more understanding. His first priority was that nothing would come between Brian and a full recovery. He was absolutely delighted to hear that he was already making such great strides and he suggested that before we said anything to Brian, we should first talk to his doctors.

The way we were.

My own favourite photograph, shows the Mayo Clinic in the background.

Even the thought of mentioning an election to Brian seemed wrong. After all here he was only two days after life-saving surgery. Was it fair to put him under the pressure of having to decide whether he would stand again or was it time for him to retire? I decided to put the whole thing out of my head until the following morning. Then, when I went across to see Brian I would have a better idea of how he was feeling and that would make up my mind whether I would tell him about the election or not. But that was not to be either...

CHAPTER FOURTEEN

When I walked in to Brian's room the next morning, I thought I would be the bearer of really sensational news for him. I couldn't believe it when he already knew the news himself. Dr. Krom had dropped in quite late the previous evening and he mentioned that he had seen news of an Irish election on television. With his Irish patient, Ruud Krom was now taking a great interest in this news. Brian's reaction to the news of an election was mixed and he seemed reluctant initially to let his name go forward. He tells this part of the story best himself.

Brian

Charlie 'phoned me with news of the election and he left it totally up to myself whether I would stand or not. He didn't want to put me under any pressure either from himself or from the party. Even though I had only one day of convalescence behind me, the issue of whether I would stand or not was a decision that I had to make very quickly. My first reaction was one of reluctance but the unanimous support that I was getting from my constituency more or less made up my mind, subject, of course to the approval of my doctors.

*Ann rang Dr. Lennon back in the Mater to seek his advice, which was reassuring to say the least. "What in the hell did he go out there and go through all that for if he's not going to stand now?" was his immediate reaction. He, of course, had been in touch with the Mayo team at all times and was quite au fait with my recovery to date. As far as Surgeon Krom and Dr. Dickson were concerned they agreed that I could stand but they emphasised that I could not take part in any campaign as such. Nor would I be allowed give any interviews out here. So I was faced with the prospect that everyone thought I should stand but that the people at home would have to campaign for me. An important **factor in reaching a final decision was that I had to get an assurance from my doctors that I would be back in Ireland for the re-***

sumption of the Dáil to vote for the Taoiseach on June 29th. There was no question of me being there any earlier than that and I was very lucky to get their approval. I had to engage in a little bit of arm-twisting because they thought I was a bit mad to be so keen.

To say that that Friday was hectic would be a gross understatement. The 'phones never stopped ringing and I was fielding them from

A surprise visit from Niall.

6

my bed. Ann was over in the hotel taking 'phone calls and Gabriel was busy too with 'phones and faxes that were coming in from the constituency. So the end product of all the consultation with the medical people and with my constituency was that I would stand. I rang the Taoiseach and told him that I was going to stand. He was delighted with my decision. I rang Brian, my son and Éamon Nolan, my Director of Elections to say that they were free to say at the convention at the West County Hotel, the following Sunday, that I was going to be a candidate. I dictated a message on the 'phone to be read out at the convention. I directed that my sons Brian and Conor would represent me. Both had their own roles, Conor in the public relations side and Brian specifically representing me. They would fit into the organisation under Éamon Nolan as Director of Elections.

So that was a very memorable Friday.

The following Sunday everything went well at the convention and I was accepted as a candidate for Dublin West again. Now with the election campaign under way my main concern was to get across to the public at home, in the country generally, and more particularly to my constituents, that the operation had been successful and that I would be fit and well to resume duties, but that I wasn't able to participate in the campaign. The key element was that I would be back home for the resumption of the Dáil on June 29th. It was vital to establish the credibility of my return. I didn't under any circumstances want to be considered a lame duck candidate and above all I was not looking for a sympathy vote. I wanted a vote on the basis of past services rendered and future services to be fulfilled. But that depended on my credibility to be in full health to represent the people properly. The main thrust of my campaign had to be to establish my credibility as a deputy and as a member of the government for my supporters. The first step in that was to get this assurance to be in the Dáil for the nomination of the Taoiseach on the following June 29th. Because I couldn't do any canvassing I had to get some message over to the constituents and I decided the most effective way to do this was to have some proper photographs taken to show me in good health, dressed, up and about and active and I had them ready for the Sunday before polling day. My colleagues at home were fighting naturally on the policy issues involved in any campaign, but I was in the unusual position that my main purpose was to reassure people that I was fit to run and to represent them. That was quite crucial because if there was any fall down in credibility regarding that, then they wouldn't vote for me. So my main task was to assure and to reassure them that I was well and fit. I was quite happy to fight the election on my own record and on the Party's record as put by my colleagues.

Phone home.

During the campaign, by now I was back at the Kahler Hotel, our suite was turned into my campaign HQ. A large part of my day was spent sitting in an armchair on the 'phone and Gabriel had a busy time bringing up all the faxes that were coming through. I had the Irish morning papers faxed through each day and they were there for me when I got up. If anything occurred to me arising out of the faxes, I would immediately 'phone them and make suggestions. In fact the six-hour time difference worked very well. I talked to the Taoiseach on an occasional basis and I talked to either Brian, Conor, Dick O' Brien or Éamon Nolan each day. That became part of the daily routine during my convalescence. At home Conor organized a very effective tele-phone link-up with amplification two days before polling day. This was a great success. I was able to speak on the telephone from Rochester, to my home in Dublin to about a hundred of my election workers and local representatives, delivering what I hoped was a vigorous mes-sage to them. Reaffirming that I was well and that I would be back in time for the opening of the Dáil I thanked them for their support. These were all the people who had been working so hard for me and who for the next two days would leave no stone unturned to have me re-elected. It was both very dramatic and emotional for Ann and myself. I'm glad to say that my next direct contact with home was the day of the count when Shane Kenny from R.T.E. got me hooked up to a live national radio election special when all my supporters and hundreds of others were present at the count. They heard me taking part in this programme, when I'd just been elected the first deputy to the 26th Dáil, topping the poll in Dublin West. I felt both proud and gratified by the result. Ann and Gabriel were my only audience during the broad-cast and they were both in tears. I was hoping I wasn't having the same effect on the people listening at home. It was totally unprepared and off the cuff, but it was a great feeling to be part of that live show.

The outcome of the election had not come as a total surprise when Shane rang, because I had been assured by Brian and by Éamon, who knew from the tallymen that I would be first to be elected. Dick O'Brien, my press secretary in Foreign Affairs, was the first to actually tell me that I had been elected. To us, over 6,000 miles away from home and in view of the trauma of the first few weeks here, this was just the most wonderful news. If I had had my way then, I would have been on the next flight back to Dublin to join in the celebrations. The rest of election day the telephone kept ringing as more news of the results filtered in. We didn't leave the suite at all that day. We had all our meals there. Of course I felt frustrated not to be there in person myself, but it was very interesting to be away from the hurly-burly too. I was able to get a good overview of the situation. Dick kept me up to date with all the latest results and I was soon aware that we were not going to get an overall majority. I was able to sit back and assess that panoramic view of the election.

Everyone at home kept in very close contact with me during the day and when it was all over and Fianna Fáil did not get our majority, it made it all the more important that I would be back in time for the 29th of June because it was quite clear that there were going to be very intricate negotiations before a government could be formed. I took the view at an early stage that it was very important that the country SHOULD have a government after the election and should not be forced into another election. In my view that would have been very damaging to the economy. All the progress that had been made depended on sustaining confidence in Ireland as a place for stable investment. I had regarded that as a great achievement of the government since 1987 and it was imperative that there be a government after the election rather than an uncertain political situation. Another General Election would have been the most highly undesirable outcome and these were the thoughts uppermost in my mind. I said this when I spoke to the Taoiseach and my colleagues between then and my return home.

CHAPTER FIFTEEN

We both thought it would be unfair not to include the trojan work during the election. Conor, who managed all the public relations end of the campaign, describes it best.

Conor

Election counting centres are not always pleasant places to be. My earliest political memory stretches back to 1973. Both my father and mother had decided as a special treat to bring me to the general election count of that year. I was ten years of age, my father was Minister for Foreign Affairs and, to my young mind at least, a demonstrably popular man. Boxes were opened and the activists devoured them with their eyes, quickly jotting down the statistical information thrown up by the ballot sheets. At the beginning of the day countrymen with cloth caps would shake my little hand and tell me the father was "home and dry." As the day wore on they became more guarded in their glances. A subtle change of mood had occurred in the counting centre. The Fianna Fáil Cumainn members in the hall became a little sheepish when they looked at me. Then I heard an opposing activist, clipboard in hand, pronounce "Lenihan's gone."

The upshot of it all was my father had lost his seat having held it for the best part of twelve years. It was incomprehensible. Before I was born he was a T.D. and a minister. The drivers of the State car were as much part of my immediate family life as anyone else. What upset me most then was the fact that he had worked so hard. The idea that others did not appreciate, as I did, the sacrifices he's made in personal and family terms to be their T.D. When in last year's General Election the Returning Officer announced that Brian Lenihan was elected on the first count with over 11,000 votes it was like an answer to a prayer. A prayer that many people make; that their life's work be recognised. My father was thousands of miles away, had been perilously ill, but now, I felt, finally appreciated. Precluded by illness from seeking votes on the doorstep, the electorate had decided to endorse the work he had done before the election campaign.

It was almost as if the wheel had turned full circle from that harrowing experience over sixteen years ago in Roscommon town. I've cried twice at election counts now, once in 1973 and again last year.

Election '89 was, as the journalist James Downey put it in his book, "all things new ", the campaign nobody needed. Least of all our family. On the 25th May the Taoiseach told the Dáil he was calling an election. Just two days before that my father had come through his liver transplant operation.

I was in London where I was working for the Belfast daily newspaper, The Irish News. On the Thursday the Taoiseach called the election, there was a lot of uncertainty. I was based in the House of Commons Press Gallery and needed desperately to know if there would be an election. I rang the government Press Secretary, P.J.Mara in the late afternoon and asked him. His reply was "You'd better get your ass back home and get your old man elected." I put down the 'phone and booked a flight home for the next morning. Back in Dublin that Friday things were chaotic. My brother Brian Jnr. was busy down in the Law Courts. There was confusion at home. Paul was in school and Anita was preparing for her Intermediate Certificate exams. For much of the time after Dad's operation he could not be disturbed. The doctors were counselling against any disturbance to his full recovery. Added to this Niall was studying for his final exams in Law at Trinity. They were difficult for him because he'd done so well in previous years and now the pressure was on to do well again. He did his exams and threw himself into the campaign immediately when they were over. He concentrated on the part of the constituency south of the river, places like Neilstown, Palmerstown and Lucan.

But that Friday Brian Jnr. was in contact with the United States. Mum and Dad had talked. They both agreed he should stand. The constituency selection convention was on the following Sunday. It was

Conor meets the Taoiseach during the campaign.

important to end the uncertainty surrounding Dad's candidacy. Brian thought we should let people know once and for all. We were thinking of ringing R.T.E. directly. But I decided instead to ring Mike Burns, the station's London editor whom I knew both as a friend and a colleague in England. R.T.E. led with the story in their 6p.m. bulletin. By the time Dad rang through on Sunday I hadn't spoken to him since his operation. We knew he was standing for election in Dublin West at this stage. The doctors had assured him that he would be ready to attend the first opening day of the Dáil following the election.

It was near tea-time when the 'phone rang upstairs, the selection convention was only an hour or so away. I picked it up and said "Hello, how are you feeling, Dad?" The reply made me laugh. "Never mind me, did Ireland win the match?" It was perhaps the most reassuring thing he could have said. I knew he was in good form. The six-hour time difference between Dublin and Minnesota meant he hadn't been able to keep up with how Ireland were doing in their World Cup qualifier against Malta. It was a beautiful sunny day in Dublin and I knew he would have loved to have been at the soccer match. I gave him the score and then searched for pen and paper to take down his statement to be read to the delegates at the selection convention.

Since I had been away in London for the last four years and was unfamiliar with the constituency organisation, Brian Jnr. was given full authority by Dad to run the campaign. During Dad's illness over the last year, he'd attended meetings on his behalf, run Clinics and knew the territory very well. It would be impossible to name all of the friends who came forward before and after the convention offering to help out in the campaign. The Fianna Fáil constituency organisation really rallied round their Tánaiste. The constituency chairman Éamon Nolan was determined at all times that the Tánaiste's interests were looked after in his absence. As ever he was, as his duty demands, neutral between the three party candidates. The campaign did not get into full swing until the Thursday, two weeks before polling day, June 15th. It was a short campaign and therefore somewhat daunting. Dublin West is the most densely populated constituency in the whole country so it did not give us a lot of time to canvass.

Brian Jnr. and I shared the organisational load. In the days before the campaign got into swing Brian visited the key activists in the constituency at their Cumann meetings. Dad's campaigns in the past always worked through the local Cumainn and it was the same this time. Personal friends who gathered at the house were sent out to link up with the Cumainn members who knew their streets and roads well. In the meantime, I got on with the business of getting literature, posters and personal messages from the Tánaiste written and pro- duced. We settled on a colour photograph of Dad with his arms in the air at an Árd Fheis when he was very sick but, strangely, looking very well. His thumbs were pointed up in a triumphant gesture. It seemed to be the most appropriate way of getting across the optimism of the man and, in a sense, what the campaign was all about.

On the doorsteps most people were friendly. When they heard I was his son, they wished him well. Even those with other political preferences wished him a speedy recovery. Both Brian Jnr. and I met several people who were on the point of tears on the doorstep. One old lady in Blanchardstown wept as she spoke to Brian Jnr. on the doorstep. Despite the warm reception we were conscious that goodwill alone does not guarantee votes on Election Day. The problems of running a campaign without the candidate being there are enormous. For a start, some of your own troops become disheartened. Brian Jnr. and I were determined from the outset to dispel any notion on the doorstep that we were in fact standing a lame duck candidate who would be too unwell to take his seat. The election doorstep can often be the occasion for cruel words. At some doors they would say that Dad would not be alive to take his seat. That he was dying, too sick to stand, or finished, were other variants on the same theme. With the health issue dominant in the campaign, the abuse could become quite personal in some cases. The health cuts had left their mark across Irish society, and left some people quite embittered. "Well for him out in the Mayo Clinic," was an occasional comment at a door.

It was regrettable to hear this kind of invective on the campaign trail. But, at another level, it was good to see that people were not afraid to express their opinions in a forthright manner. After all, that's what elections are all about. It was easy to become exasperated, though, with voters who felt he could not be fit enough to perform his job when he came back from the States. One voter suggested to Brian Jnr. that it was time he hung up his boots. "Do you want to be the one who hangs them up for him?" came Brian's reply, and he walked away from the door. There was an undercurrent of doubt in some voters' minds on Dad's health. That's why, from the beginning, we briefed canvassers as fully as we could on Dad's condition so they could counter at the doors. We made only one promise to the voters in Dublin West. He was making a great recovery and would be back to vote on the first day that the Dáil reassembled after the election. At another level, canvassers had to be told how he was because there were so

Victory.

many well-wishers at the doors asking how he was. They knew the activists from the area, and expected, rightly, that they should know. At times, it became almost automatic. A door would open, we would introduce ourselves, and then the question, "How is he ?" The heartening thing was that many people who had never even met the man were voting for him because they respected the fact that he had given so many of his years to politics. More heartening because too many people are cynical about politicians and their worth.

In many ways, the campaign and Dad's illness were hardest on Anita, the youngest in the family. She was doing her Intermediate Certificate, her first set of serious exams. A front room in the house had been converted into an impromptu campaign headquarters. New 'phone lines were in and ringing incessantly at all hours of the day and *night. Added to that there were people walking in and out all day. Luckily, good friends came forward and offered to let Anita stay with them at weekends. They had a daughter doing the exams too. But it meant Anita was distant from the campaign, which I'm sure she was anxious about. Paul was in fifth year, and doing his school summer exams. He opted to stay at home. When he finished them, he came out to canvass, something he had never done before. Poetry rather than politics is his big interest. Given his years and lack of previous experience, we were surprised how calm and effective he was with voters twice his age.*

As polling day got closer, the campaign was in full swing. The troops were slightly disheartened, despite the good news of Dad's rapid recovery in the States, that there were no newspaper interviews with him and Mum. While we knew he was well from his many calls and inquiries about the campaign, it was difficult to convey this on. There was no shortage of requests for interviews from the media. Charlie Bird from R.T.E. television was ready to get on a plane and go out to Minnesota, as were others from the newspapers. It was difficult to explain that despite his recovery, the doctors out there felt it was important that he should not be allowed to get too involved in the campaign by giving interviews. In the end, after some debate, it was agreed that some local photographer from Minnesota would take a picture of Mum and Dad to be sent back for the Sunday papers before polling day. The physical evidence of how he was doing really buoyed up spirits and lifted the campaign. All three Sunday newspapers carried stories, with two of them using the pictures.

Traditionally, there is no canvassing on the eve of polling day. It's a time to settle down and prepare for the next day. People have to be assigned polling booths, transport arranged to bring the voters to the stations, and food prepared for those who are spending the whole day on their feet. A good friend decided to provide a 'phone with a public address system built in. All of those who had been out canvassing and who had helped out were asked to come to the house. Dad rang up from Minnesota and first spoke privately to the local councillors, each one in turn, thanking them for their help. It was the first time they had spoken to him since his departure to the States. Then he rang back on the 'phone downstairs. There were nearly a hundred people crammed into the front room which doubled as campaign headquarters. Dad's voice came over loud and clear. Thanking them all, he spoke about the issues in the campaign. He had been following it closely with cuttings from the newspapers faxed out to him throughout the two weeks. It was an emotional gathering. There were people there who had worked with Dad since he first came to the constituency, and others who knew him since he was a very young man. Tears were welling up in the eyes of those who had given freely of their time throughout this campaign and many others down the years. Dad told them of the need for stable government to consolidate the economic achievement of the past two years. Though on the other side of the Atlantic, he might as well have been there with us in the room. It was a Brian Lenihan speech. Only at the end, when he was finished, and thanking everybody again, could one detect a certain emotion in his voice. He said that both he and Mum were very grateful and aware that none of this could have happened without their supporters. Somebody broke into song, and everybody sang "For He's a Jolly Good Fellow" back at him in Minnesota. When the 'phone was put down we were very sorry that we had forgotten to tape it all.

Thankfully, polling day was sunny. There were no problems, with everybody in place for the final push. Brian Jnr. toured the polling booths, taking up the duties of the absent candidate. Sometimes there is friction between candidates on polling day, but there were no problems this time. The reports from the activists at the booths were all very positive. Some of our campaign team were predicting a surge of support for Dad, but both Brian Jnr. and I discounted this. We honestly felt he would get about the same as he got the last time out.

The count saw us pleasantly surprised. Dad was the first T.D. to be returned to Leinster House in the new Dáil. The high point of the day was his live interview from the United States. Brian Jnr. was in the R.T.E. radio studio talking live in a link-up with Minnesota. On the floor of the counting centre, a huddle of supporters were crowded around a man holding a small transistor over his head. They were smiling at his every word. As a moment, it seemed to sum up the devotion and loyalty of those who'd helped out over the campaign. We had been as good as our promise during the campaign. Our candidate would walk into Leinster House in better condition than before and ready to serve.

CHAPTER SIXTEEN

Brian's rapid recovery was nothing short of a miracle. From the time of his operation he never looked back. Even by the Mayo Clinic's standards, all his medical staff said his recovery was quite remarkable. On the Friday after his operation he was well enough to attend the weekly counselling session. Dr. Krom was giving the lecture that day and Conor came along with us. It happened that this particular lecture dealt with the liver operation in minute detail. I was wondering what the effect of the lecture would be on Brian. In the normal course of events he would have attended that lecture prior to his own surgery, but with the speed at which everything happened in the end, here he was with his own operation over.

Back in the hotel.

His friends from the Transplant Unit, Tom Jorgenson from Iowa and Sally Hauser from Ohio couldn't believe it when he arrived into the lecture room. Tom was still hospitalized nearly three months after his transplant and Sally was awaiting hers. She was especially delighted with Brian's recovery. She said that it gave her great hope for herself. All the transplant patients were so friendly. It was a tightly-knit group of caring people who felt bound together by the miracle that the Mayo Clinic could work for them. We heard that at other transplant centres there was quite a bit of tension between the transplant patients as they kept track of who was where on the waiting list, in case anyone might jump the queue. By comparison Mayo was like an extended family.

After ten days Brian was discharged from the hospital and he was back in the Kahler hotel again, from where he conducted his election campaign. I have no doubt that the challenge to be home for the reopening of the Dáil provided him with a fantastic stimulus to recover. We had two days of testing at the Clinic each week and these tended to be all-day affairs and were very tiring for both of us. His medication was constantly monitored during this period, but it too was stabilized very quickly.

We had some pleasant outings during our last days in Rochester. One evening we went out to Michael and Rebecca Brennan's house for dinner. Michael's Dad, Colm, and his mum, Anna, were out from Dublin for a visit so it was great to catch up on all the election news from them. Another afternoon we had a really rousing sing-song over in the hospital. Tom Jorgensen was a great pianist and the nurses arranged to have a piano brought up to the 5th floor to help Tom's recuperation. Tom played all the old favourites and Brian sang some Irish songs. It was a bitter-sweet occasion. We were sad to be leaving behind these good friends and we were equally sad to be leaving the medical team who had surpassed our wildest expectations, not only as the ultimate practitioners of such highly specialized medicine, but as thoroughly caring individuals.

Musical interlude with Tom Jorgensen and Sally Hauser.

Singing along with Tom and Jane Jorgensen.

Me and my Teddybear.

Farewell festivities with Peter Gunning, Dr. John Lennon and Gabriel.

We got used to rambling around the small town and we were very taken by the friendliness of everyone we met. One day we took Brian on a shopping spree. He bought a couple of Western shirts, a pair of jeans and a couple of pairs of loafers. We called it his Mid-West look. In the shoe shop the young man who was serving us recognized Brian from an article about him that had appeared in the local paper. " You're the Prime Minister of Ireland or something aren't you?" he asked. Brian was quite chuffed to be recognized here in his newly adopted town. However when we got back to the hotel he was annoyed to say the least when he discovered that he had left one pair of shoes behind him. Some time later a parcel was delivered up to our room addressed to the Prime Minister of Ireland. The enterprising young man had taken the trouble to find out where we were staying and he delivered the shoes around to the hotel himself. In a way that gesture said more about the town and the people than anything I could describe.

During our stay at the hotel we were inundated with Get Well cards, Masses and good wishes not only from friends and colleagues at home, but also, we received stacks of mail from local people in Rochester. They sent us small gifts and nice notes saying how pleased they were that Brian had come to their town for his operation. One afternoon Brian arrived back from the Clinic with a big smile on his face. Under his arm was the famous Ruud Krom teddy bear. The white teddy with the smart red bow has become Dr. Krom's trademark. He gives one to all his transplant patients when they are about to return home. While the doctors were all pleased with Brian's recovery, they would have preferred if he could have stayed on in Rochester for another couple of weeks. But it would have taken a very brave army to try to come between Brian and the opening of the new Dáil. The arrival of teddy meant that our stay at Rochester was coming to an end. Within days we had been given a date for our return home to Dublin. The red letter day was June 26th, which would have us home two days before the opening of the 26th Dáil.

Our last weekend was particularly memorable because Niall, who had been working in Boston, flew to join us in Rochester. He looked tanned and healthy which delighted both of us and we were very pleased that he had passed his finals with flying colours and had won a place in Cambridge for his post-graduate degree.

The night before we left Rochester we had a going-away party at a nearby restaurant. Peter Gunning, the Consul General from Chicago, flew down for the evening and Dr. John Lennon flew out from the Mater to be briefed by the Mayo team. He spent a long day consulting with them and returned to the hotel armed with what looked like tons of Brian's files to be brought back to the Mater. We didn't have a late night because we knew we had an early start the following morning. Our departure was set for 9.00 a.m.

We still had to face the dreaded packing. Brian had accumulated such an amount of newspapers and magazines and of course

Packing up.

Up, up and away.

Pilot Brian.

when you are away from home for an extended stay you gather so much extra baggage. But eventually with the aid of extra suitcases everything was sorted out. I hardly slept a wink that last night because I was so excited. We were up at the crack of dawn on our last day. After a quick breakfast our car arrived to take us to the airport. Once there we were quickly on board the Jet and were bound for Dublin. With a stop to refuel at Goose Bay, we arrived back in Dublin just before ten that same evening. We felt quite overcome by the great welcome we got. In addition to the family, Noel Dorr and his wife, Catriona, Orla O' Hanrahan and our two drivers Tom Lyons and Jim Lynagh were there on the tarmac. Also there to welcome us were the doctors from the Mater and Catherine Butler from the Taoiseach's office. It was hard to believe it was happening. We had finally arrived back home. Brian was admitted to the Mater that night simply to check that everything was alright. The following day he arrived back home to a hero's welcome in Castleknock.

Shortly after 10.00 on Thursday June 29th, the car arrived to take us to Leinster House. It was a beautiful sunny day and almost as warm as the weather we had got used to in Rochester. At the door of Government Buildings, the Taoiseach was waiting to welcome Brian back to work. It was a great reunion for the two old friends. Then it was over to Leinster House where Brian received a standing ovation from all sides of the House. The rapturous applause seemed to go on forever. Everyone seemed genuinely happy to see him back in their midst. It was a magic moment, one that I wouldn't have even dared to dream of only a few short weeks before. I was overcome with happiness, and I was also proud that Brian had been as good as his word. He had kept his promise to his constituents and was back in better condition than before ready to serve. All the prayers had been answered.

Welcome home.

Great to be back, Boss.

"Take it from me ..." to Seamus Brennan.

CHAPTER SEVENTEEN

Brian

It's hard to describe the gratitude I felt to everyone at the Mayo Clinic, and indeed to the good people of Rochester, who had constantly wished us well during our stay. But I have to admit that I was raring to get home and back into the Dáil. I suppose that in itself summed up my recovery. My doctors had agreed to my early discharge from their care because they understood that all I had to do on my return home was to go into the Dáil to vote. Then with the benefit of the summer recess, I would have plenty of time at home in Castleknock and over in the West to continue my convalescence. It all sounded like music to my ears. Events, however, were not to facilitate that original plan.

I was quite overwhelmed by the ovation I got from all sides of the House when I arrived to propose Charlie as Taoiseach of the 26th Dáil. The rest is now history. Fianna Fáil lost that vote and we found ourselves in the position of being unable to elect a new Taoiseach. The outgoing government remained in office, and the Dáil was adjourned for discussions to take place on how the impasse could be resolved.

What followed was a very difficult period in which there were numerous meetings of the Government, the Parliamentary Party and the National Executive, and of course the business of the Government, running the country, had to proceed as well. It was quite clear at an early stage that there was no way in which the Dáil would support Fianna Fáil as a minority government. We could not negotiate ourselves into that. The alternative on offer from Alan Dukes was a 50% participation in Government by Fine Gael, with Mr. Dukes as the rotating Taoiseach. This was so obviously tongue in cheek that it was never a runner. Dick Spring and The Workers' Party had decided to renege on any participation. They had adopted a posture of isolating themselves on the Left, as they described it.

Anita, Daddy's girl.

On the G.B. Show.

So when Fine Gael, Labour and The Workers' Party, for practical purposes, reneged on their responsibilities about governing the country, the options open to us were limited. We could have ceased further effort to form a government, in which event there would have been another General Election. As I've already said, in my view this would have been disastrous for the country. I remained personally strongly opposed to another election. The one thing we had earned for the country was the high degree of confidence among the investing community both at home and abroad in the stability of Ireland as an economy. As a country that was going places, all of this would be destroyed by any retreat to a Banana Republic status of frequent elections. I did feel very strongly about that.

In practical terms, as the days went on, it emerged that the only real prospect of forming a government was an alliance with the P.D.s, who numbered six and who would just give us the required majority. This

Back at the office.

of course gave rise to tensions within our own party because of the fairly recent nature of the breakaway of leading P.D. members from our party. Again because the national interest was at stake, I felt very strongly that we should try to forget about personalities. After all we had worked in Government before with leading people from the P.D.s, O' Malley and Molloy. Although acrimonious things had been said since the P.D.s were formed, the fact of the matter was that the national interest should now predominate. I felt that the electorate had made their decision and that we should try to form a government within the parameters of their decision. The circumstances logically led to some kind of an alliance with the P.D.s; otherwise there would be chaos.

So the negotiations with the P.D.s commenced, handled by Albert Reynolds and Bertie Ahern who were dealing with Bobby Molloy and Pat Cox. They reported back to the government at all stages. The

Targetting Defence.

Taoiseach and O' Malley had meetings as well. The National Executive and the Parliamentry Party had meetings, and then the Dáil met once during that period also. That two-week period seemed to be a succession of meetings and from the moment I left the house in Castleknock early in the morning, it was non-stop until near midnight. I'd hate to think what my doctors in Mayo would have had to say about their patient. But there was an important job to be done and I wanted to see a constructive outcome for the country. But it was an exhausting period for me because I had come back from the States, before my time almost. I had asked the doctors to let me back early, pushing the thing to the limit to let me home on time. I got back on the assurance to them that the meeting of the Dáil would be a mere formality. I didn't foresee the stalemate situation, that meant instead of a one-day meeting in the Dáil, we were facing two weeks of numerous meetings, which eventually resulted in the P.D.s agreeing to go into Government with us on the basis of two ministers in the Government and Mary Harney as a Junior Minister.

When the Dáil met two weeks later, I proposed Charlie as Taoiseach of the 26th Dáil and he was duly elected.. Once that job was done, I knew my own limitations. I was tired from the days of non-stop political activity. My return to politics had been a bit of an ordeal and my health had been severely tested. While I was delighted to have played a role in the formation of the new government, I was also aware of the need now to pace myself. So I booked into the Mater that evening. I was not in a position technically to receive the Seal of Office as Minister for Defence that night but the Taoiseach took it from the President on my behalf. I spent a week recuperating in the Mater and I came out restored to good health again and ready to take on my duties.

All together now.

At the Garden Of Remembrance.

Stepping out.

Glasnost with Genadi Uranov, The Soviet Ambassador.

Those April Showers that come my way, with Gerry Collins and Tom King.

With Eoin Maguire from Clontarf, lighting a candle for the Cystic Fibrosis Association National Candle Day.

EPILOGUE

Our return to Rochester on New Year's Day this year could not have been in starker contrast to our last visit. Having thoroughly enjoyed Christmas with our family, we were still in a festive mood when we landed at the small airport. This time we brought Anita with us. It was her first visit to the United States and she had been avidly looking forward to it. As we flew in over the prairies, it was a magical scene, like something out of a story book. As far as the eye could see, a thick blanket of snow covered the ground. That special, rather haunting light that reflects from the snow made everything seem skeletal in appearance. We arrived back to the Kahler Hotel, where Kevin Molloy had been thoughtful enough to give us the same Suite 1,000 we had before. And there was an Irish welcome waiting for us too. A Christmas card from Kevin and his wife Cinta, and some Irish Christmas cake made by Cinta herself.

Anita was in a nearby room. I was delighted to have her with us because I wanted her to see the Mayo Clinic and the hospital which played such a large part in our lives. I hoped it would also help to finally lay the ghost about her father's illness. During the week, she saw all over the hospital and the Clinic and she learned a lot about liver transplantation.

This time everything was totally different. Instead of the searing heat and humidity of the summer, we were now experiencing the flip-side of the weather coin, sub-zero temperatures. Now, I was able to fully appreciate those heated subways. Since Brian was having some trouble with his leg, it was easy to wheel him across to the Clinic. The day started very early for us. First appointments were at 6.00 a.m. at the 11th floor West, in the Clinic. Brian was usually fasting for the first tests so we returned to the hotel Coffee Shop for breakfast about 10.00 where Anita would be waiting for us. Then it was back to continue more tests until lunchtime. After lunch there was another heavy schedule ahead of Brian. His doctors there felt that since they had him for a few days, they wanted to give him a really thorough testing. Some evenings we did not get back to our room in the hotel until well after seven. On those evenings I was so tired that I flopped down on the bed and fell fast asleep, without having any dinner. On the other nights, we had dinner in the hotel. I don't know how Brian kept up with the pace because some of the others we met who were undergoing the same tests seemed really ill as a result of them.

For the first few days we didn't meet any of the staff we had known during our previous stay. The Registrars rotate every six months as they continue their studies. The ones we would have known would now be possibly at the Heart Transplant unit at St. Mary's. When we met Dr. Krom and Dr. Dickson, they were both extremely pleased with Brian's progress. We asked about the other transplant patients we had known during our first visit. Tom Jorgensen had finally gone home to Iowa after 109 days in convalescence at the hospital. He had a number of set-backs after his operation, which again highlighted for us just how miraculous Brian's recovery had been. The very sad news was that our good friend Sally Hauser, who received the transplant immediately after Brian, had died just before Christmas. The doctors were very sad about Sally. They said that she had the same attitude as Brian about the operation and was always very gutsy. She had returned home to Ohio and just before the three month post-operation mark, she had developed complications. Dr. Dickson wanted to send the Mayo Clinic jet to bring her back to the hospital, but she had declined. It seems she wanted to die at home.

The only tiny cloud on our horizon was Brian's leg which had been causing him a considerable amount of pain for the previous seven months. At the Clinic they suggested we see an orthopaedic surgeon and get his opinion. He decided to put the leg in a cast for two months, in order to give it a better chance to heal. Because

of his medication, Brian is a slow healer. It was a small price to pay for the glowing medical report he received from Dr. Dickson when he finally got finished that Friday. We immediately rang Dr. John Lennon at the Mater to tell him the good news.

That Friday evening Rolly Dickson hosted a dinner for us at the hotel. He invited the Irish doctors and their wives who had been kind to us in May. It was nice to meet Colum and Una Gorman, Michael O'Sullivan and Margaret, Des O'Duffy and his daughter who was such good company for Anita, and Dan and Ruth Connolly. Brian Spain, Brian's Private Secretary in Defence also joined us. It was a really great evening and turned into a right old Irish hooley before the night was out. Michael O'Sullivan, like all Kerrymen, was a great musician. He brought his guitar and regaled us with old Irish songs, many he had learned from his grandmother. They were really beautiful, many of them we had never heard before. Rolly Dickson entered into the spirit of the celebration and sang a number of his old Fraternity songs from his college days. Brian kept the Lenihan family flag flying by singing his own favourite The Star of The County Down. It was a very memorable evening.

The next day we had time to relax. I took Anita out to the Apache Mall, a new shopping centre just a few miles outside the town. That evening Kevin and Cinta Molloy, Michael and Rebecca Brennan and Brendan and Mary Moore joined us for dinner. We finished early that evening because we wanted to get some rest before our flight the following morning. Before we left we paid a visit to the little chapel on the third floor of the hospital. We were sorry to miss the chaplain who had been kindness itself to Brian. On Sunday morning, shortly after 8.00a.m. our flight took off from Rochester. With Brian beside me, chatting and laughing with Anita, we could have been any family off on a trip. But I am well aware that we are now a very special family and I thank God for it.

Brian

On January 5th 1990 I finished my recheck tests with Dr. Rolland Dickson in the Mayo Clinic. Back in my room at the Kahler Hotel I reread a copy of his report to my doctors in the Mater.

" I was gratified to see how very well Brian Lenihan had done during this six month post-transplantation examination. He now has normal liver function tests. "

I focused on the last sentence. So it was over. The disciplined way of life, which I now enjoyed, would continue, but otherwise it was over. I looked from my window at the dusk settling over the vast prairie rolling past Rochester from the Mississippi to the Black Hills, where the Sioux Indians had chased buffalo over the centuries, and I thought. I was privileged and thankful The Good Lord had loved me, Ann had minded me, and thousands had prayed for me. Modern medicine and its practitioners had saved me. So be it. I thought of the daily fight every person faces in the ongoing battle of life, of the need to sustain the human spirit, that is, because it thinks, and believes in the resurrection of the self same spirit after every adversity.

I thought of St. Paul (Romans 8: 31-39):

"Who can be against us if God is on our side? He did not even spare his own Son, but gave Him up for us all..." and his conclusions: "Of this I am fully persuaded; Neither death nor life, neither what is present, nor what is to come, no force whatever will be able to separate us from the love of God, which comes to us in Christ Jesus Our Lord."

It is all there.